AF615588

Stefan Gec

Stefan Gec

Andrew Patrizio

Edited by Jon Bewley

Contexts and Strategies **13**
Introduction 14
The Biographical Context 20
Strategies of the Artist 26
Under Pressure **35**
Fædm 36
Fragment / Vengeance 42
Decompression Chamber 54
Half Lives and Whole Worlds **59**
Fallout from Chernobyl 60
Bitter Waters 68
Natural History 72
Trace Elements 80
Detached Bell Tower 88
Buoy 92
Towards a New Public Domain **102**
Notes **103**

Contexts and Strategies

Introduction

... we should begin by acknowledging that the map of the world has no divine or dogmatically sanctioned spaces, essences or privileges... human experience is finely textured, dense, and accessible enough *not* to need extra-historical or extra-worldly agencies to illuminate or explain it. I am talking about a way of regarding our world as amenable to investigation and interrogation without magic keys, special jargons and instruments, curtained-off practices.[1]

Buoy, 1996 (ongoing)
Maritime Museum,
Hartlepool

All artists have to work within the determinants of his or her time: the conditions of possibility that have an effect on what can be thought and imagined, what can be made, what can be sold and what can be seen by others. Some artists today work in ways which their ancient predecessors might recognise, whether it be through the routines of a studio, the existence of a supportive gallery and collecting structure, or the availability of a known audience. But if your work as an artist relies on a deep engagement with the worlds beyond art (art as art), as is the case with Stefan Gec, then the determinants of your time and the conditions of possibility are inevitably different from a number of your counterparts. In order to address the creative and imaginative moments that make up the story of Stefan Gec's career so far, we must begin to mark out some of the contours of the world, at least as they might appear to a contemporary artist such as Gec.

Gec works as an artist within Western culture yet through his father has immediate family ties to Eastern, pre-industrial Europe. Though, this very familiar, formative fact – the binary situation that existed between East and West Europe, indeed the Eastern and Western worlds – is virtually dead history or at least in drastic need of revision. As the American/Lebanese historian Edward Said has written, "Gone are the binary oppositions dear to the nationalist and imperialist enterprise. Instead, we begin to sense that old authority cannot simply be replaced by new authority, but that new alignments made across borders, types, nations, and essences are rapidly coming into view, and it is those new alignments that now provoke and challenge the fundamentally static notion of *identity* that has been the core of cultural thought during the era of imperialism."[2] The key phrase here is "new alignments", as Said tries to plot a new world in which everything is becoming realigned over time – power structures, economic fortunes and speculative ventures come and go. The world is never static and 'finished', but always in movement between one state and another. Every city, for example, has a unique identity that can no more be contained within its administrative borders, as it can within its buildings, its racial mix, or the kind of food one can buy on its streets.

Rather these places have names of convenience, and are porous, changing systems, or a series of systems, bound together along certain lines of power and organisation which, however strong, break down and alter over time. This breakage, alteration and subsequent reformation happens because of the interactions that inevitably take place in the course of living out our lives in social space. We are rightly starting to think more seriously about the processual and ongoing dynamic that moves everything along, inevitably yet indeterminately, and hold less dear the static artefacts and end products that used to be seen as originating only from bounded territories. Similarly,

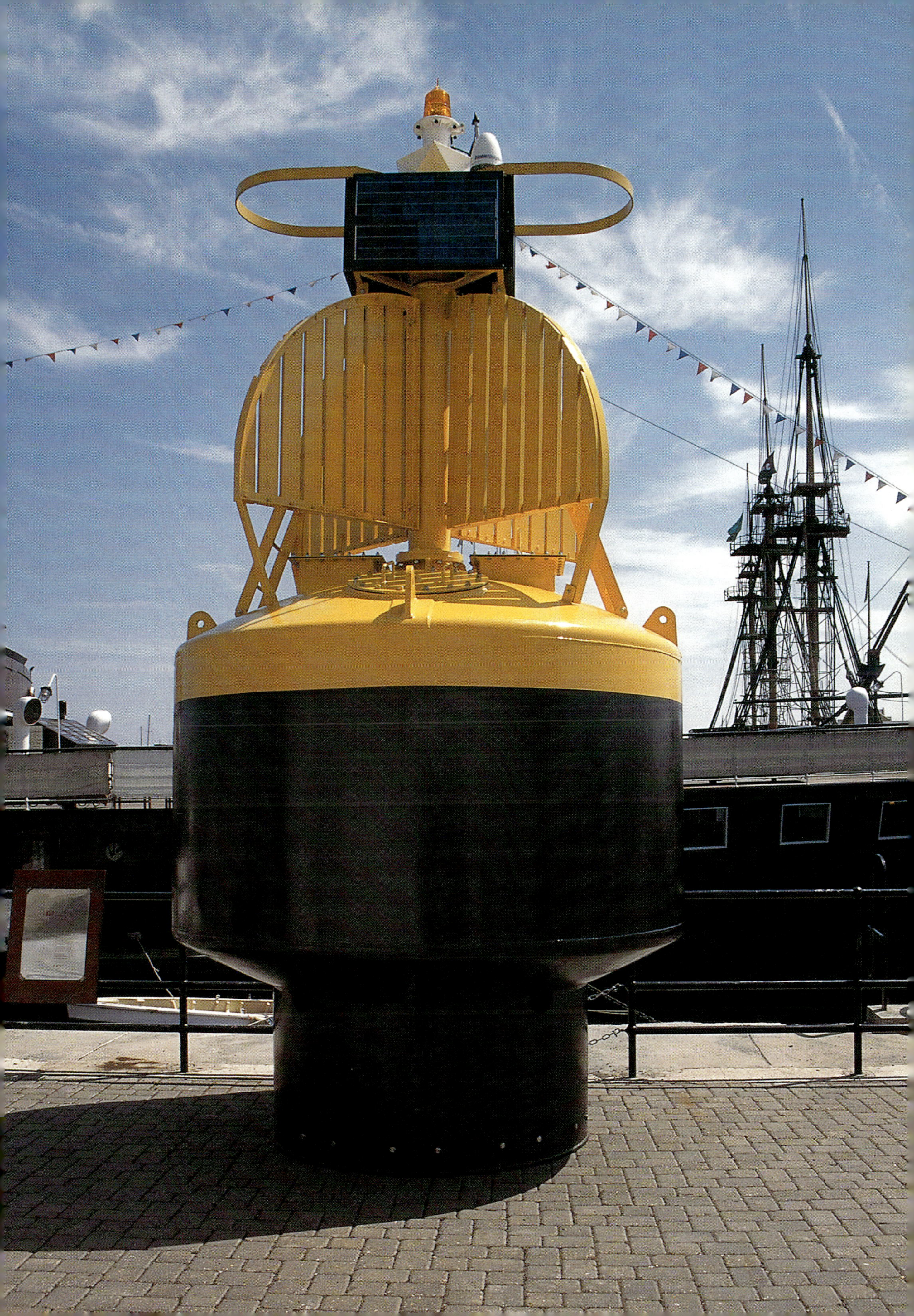

the creation of an ethnically pure past can be seen to be little more than a holding operation by power groups seeking to establish an exclusion zone of authenticity and lineage against 'corruption' from outside; and whether that is viewed benignly or negatively depends on how one views the operation of power within that context. Our notion of 'community' can be sympathetically filmed in soft focus or savagely reinforced by violence.

Another perspective on the "new alignments" that Said talks of is illustrated by the fiscal future of Western Europe, as it currently reorganises its currency in ways that are remarkable and unequalled anywhere else in the world. Such tectonic changes, resulting in the voluntary erasure of national monies, would have been difficult to predict even ten years ago. Not only are new languages and methods of discourse required to match the new situation, but as a consequence, new ways of acting, of creating, become possible and reflect the difference. How do artists find a mode of working that is still intelligible to a population whose cultural and economic co-ordinates are shifting? And how sensitive to location is it possible to be, when boundaries are no longer (never were) a fixed feature of our world?

We live, particularly but not exclusively, in an increasingly poly-vocal culture where the fields of communication and exchange hum with electronic noise. It has become a commonplace that there is more *quantity* of communication, if you like, but certainly less clarity in the space between those who communicate. One of the roles of the artist today, when communities only really connect with each other in an essentially 'imagined' way, might be to create plausible and alternative junctions that mark important points in our cultural and psychological landscape. Through them, other connections can be brought to life, not just within art but as part of the political and economic worlds we inhabit.

Imperialism after all is an act of geographical violence through which virtually every space in the world is explored, charted, and finally brought under control. For the native, the history of colonial servitude is inaugurated by the loss of the locality to the outsider; its geographical identity must thereafter be searched for and somehow restored. Because of the presence of the colonizing outsider, the land is recoverable at first only through the imagination.[3]

If the conjunction of the powerful and the vulnerable is a political fact that helps to create a context for looking at Gec's work, then so is the existence of the nomad, the refugee and the emigrant. Forced travel undertaken, for example, by political or economic refugees fleeing internal conflict is a phenomenon that serves to disperse individuals, cultures and communities. This phenomenon, which might roughly be termed 'transnationalism', directly impinged on Gec's family and provided a powerful impetus to his art practice as it emerged, with works like *Buoy*, 1996 (ongoing). Those who flee or choose to move, under conditions that offer few alternatives often have no final destination in mind, and travel under duress, leaving most of their belongings behind them. They leave but they do not yet arrive. Their mobility is also curtailed by policed borders, international law and the willingness or otherwise of politicians elsewhere to allow influxes of those from outside into the social and cultural fabric of the host. To take a recent example of forced hybridity and how bizarre ethnic identities can be constructed, consider the plight of the Afghan and other refugees denied access to Australia (in the lead-up to national elections in 2001) who, after days at the centre of a complex international incident, were finally allowed to land in the region of Papua New Guinea, where a welcoming party greeted these sorry political migrants. Assuming that a number of the Afghans will stay on the island and make a life for themselves in South East Asia, new individuals and cultures will be created from political circumstances one could hardly imagine possible.

In the context of such a dizzyingly complex world, it becomes almost impossible to assert an easy correlation between a nation, a people and its culture. As Swedish sociologist Ulf Hannerz describes, there is too much cross-contamination, movement and hybridity for purity to stand a chance. "As people move with their meanings, and as meanings find ways of travelling even when people stay put, territories cannot really contain cultures. And even as one accepts that culture is socially acquired and organized, the assumption that it is homogeneously distributed within collectivities becomes problematic, when we see how their members' experiences and biographies differ."[4] So, the existence of clearly defined communities, be they based on ethnic origin, gender or religious belief, is not as closed, bounded or authentically pure as might be imagined. Similarly, such communities do not function in a fixed geographic place. People create communities for themselves and through their own social interactions person to person, family to family or group to group. Social space and a sense of community is not a physical thing out there – a sculptural metaphor – but is formed out of the myriad points of contact, collaborations, exchanges and those spaces in-between.

Gec's work, as we will see, looks forward to the new patterns that are appearing in our culture. However, it also looks back, and draws on the power of the industrial, technological and architectural spheres which were founded on utopianism and universality. The 1950s, as Britain's heavy industries faced an increasingly uncertain future, saw the rise of the new specialism of industrial archaeology as a conservationist and rearguard response to that decline. Gec's work establishes an alternative to the investment in industrial museums and nostalgic publications based on oral reminiscences and old photographs; he has worked with industrial artefacts that have long been beyond use, and has further transformed their function from melancholic memory to objects of poetic resilience.

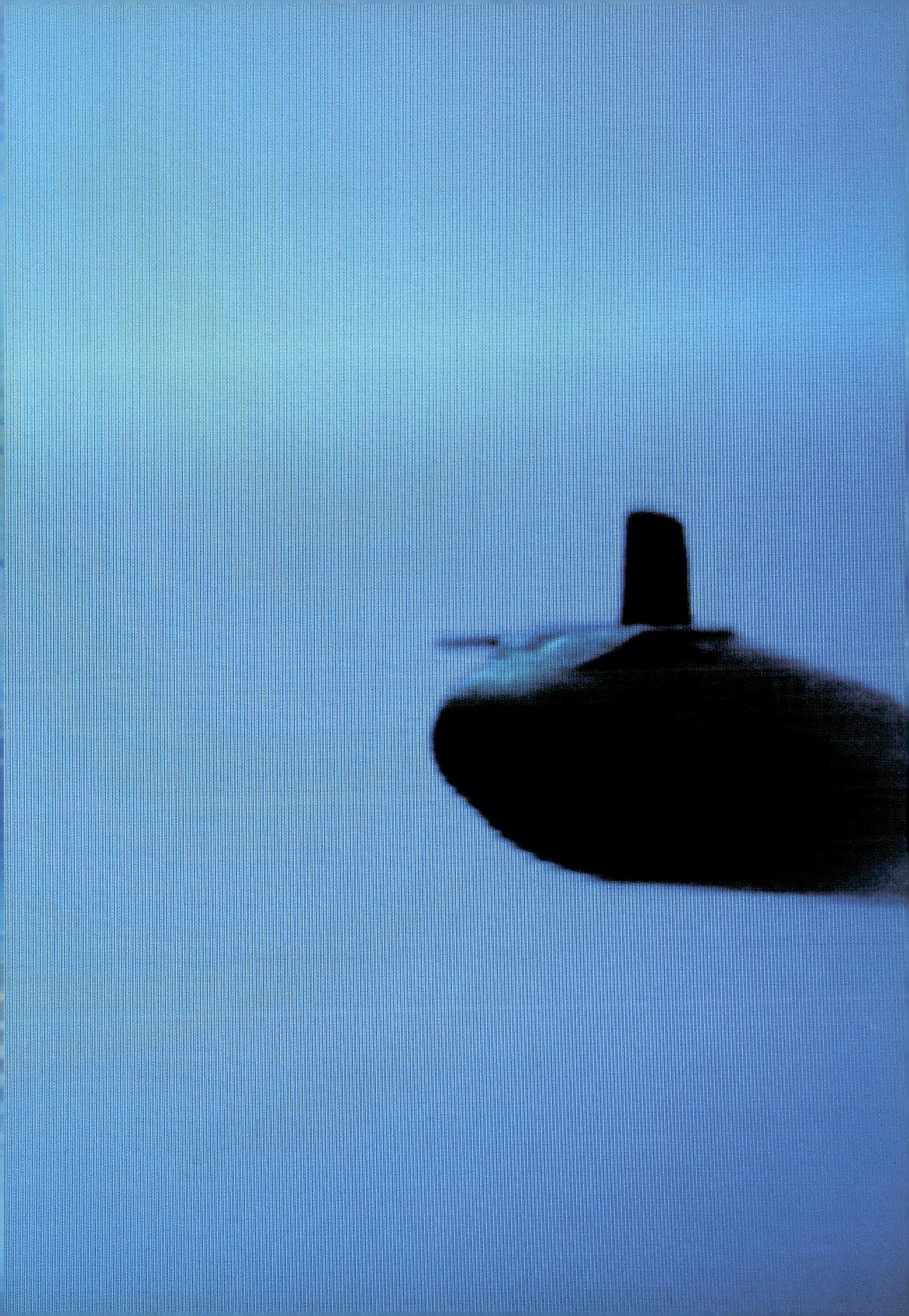

The Biographical Context

It is significant both to aspects of Gec's art and his life, that his family history reflects the reality of transnational migration across Europe and America. His immediate family in Ukraine have, over the first half of the twentieth century, been forced, or have chosen, to move from their homeland; some have moved through political upheaval, others through economic necessity, but whatever the circumstances (some of which will be described below) the Gec family experience is a microcosm of twentieth century cultural dispersal and mobility. Gec's venture into his Ukrainian lineage was motivated in part by his feelings of insecurity in an orthodox fine art educational system and by genuine curiosity concerning his own identity.

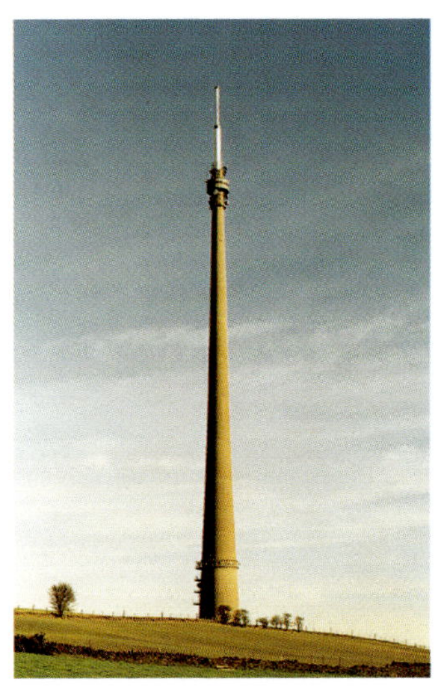

Emley Moor Transmission Mast, West Yorkshire

After spending seven years as an unskilled worker in a textile mill in Huddersfield, Gec became an art student and it took him only a matter of weeks to start to explore his Ukrainian background through art. What began with modest etchings has become the engine of his subsequent creativity. For Gec it was his incomplete and vague knowledge of his father's homeland which spurred his further enquiry and he admits that if his father had bombarded him with stories from the East it may well have extinguished his own curiosity. Relative silence allowed multiple narratives and possibilities to grow in his own mind. He does, however, remember a strong atmosphere in the childhood home over the Cold War period when conflicts within the Eastern Bloc, particularly Russia's moves on Ukraine, were felt sharply by Gec's father. A characteristic that the artist now feels is important in a wider context: artworks, and their explanation should never offer immediate gratification but, through fragmentary revelation, become increasingly powerful over time.

Appropriately enough, 'Ukraine' roughly translates as 'borderland', lying as it does to the far south west of Russia and most of her other 'Republics'. Ukraine along with Belarus is ethnically East Slav and used to be under the control of Lithuania and Poland, and their Roman Catholic ruling classes. More romantically, it is the original Cossack country. In the twentieth century, this area suffered many major disruptions to its ethnic and cultural shape, firstly through Hitler's drive east in the middle years of the Second World War (at which time Gec's father was sent by the Germans as a labourer to Austria, followed a year later by Gec's grandfather to Germany). Shortly after the War and leaving little time for recovery, Stalin had millions killed or deported to work in the Gulags. Because of this Gec's family were fearful of returning home. Around the same time, his grandmother and her remaining children also fled their homeland. After the War his grandfather emigrated to the US and his father eventually arrived, via Austria, in the UK; first to Lincoln then Huddersfield, where many other Ukrainians struck down roots. Such convoluted family history is not unusual in recent times, of course, but is still emotive and dramatic, marking Gec's family clearly as reluctant and dispersed emigrants.

In this context one can cite a photographic work by the artist, *Control Tower*, 1995, which drew on his father's earliest experiences in this country. *Control Tower* is a work inspired by the former Royal Air Force base at Wigsley near Lincoln, which was used as a refugee camp for internees during the Second World War. The artist's father was interned there for a short time just after the end of the War, thinking he would be returned home shortly. Although now derelict, the remains of a three-storey control tower and runway still exist.

For *Control Tower* homing pigeons, with small cameras attached to their breasts, were released nearby and the shutters automatically released when the birds were directly above the base. After repeated flights an overall aerial picture emerged from the resultant photographs. (The technique of using cameras strapped to pigeons was used in the First World War as a surveillance technique to record and track troop movements). What on the surface seems a rather abject and odd sequence of black and white images is transformed by this contextual information into a delicate and subtle photo-work that draws in themes of memory, history, migration, accident and war.

Control Tower, 1995
Former RAF base at Wigsley, Lincolnshire
Photographs taken by using pigeons fitted with miniature cameras

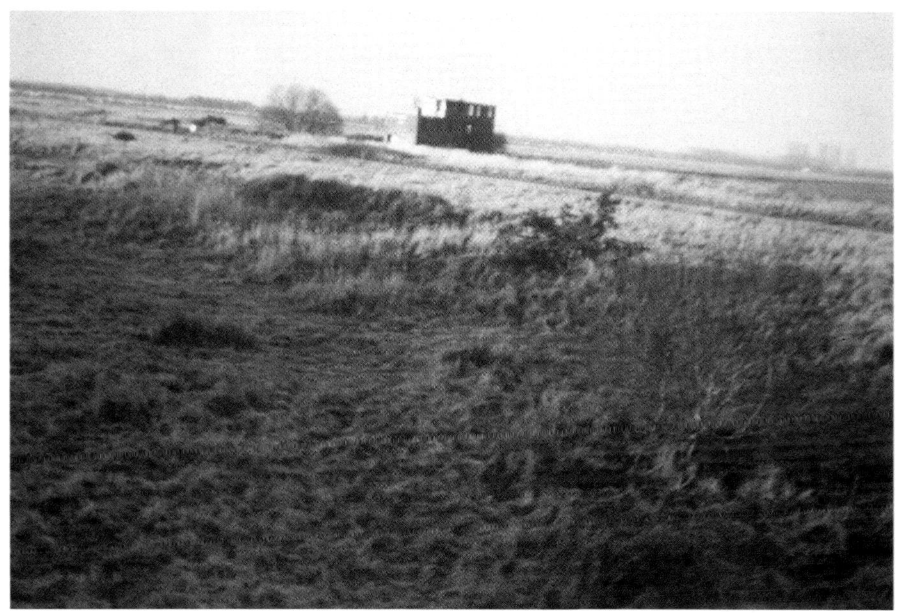

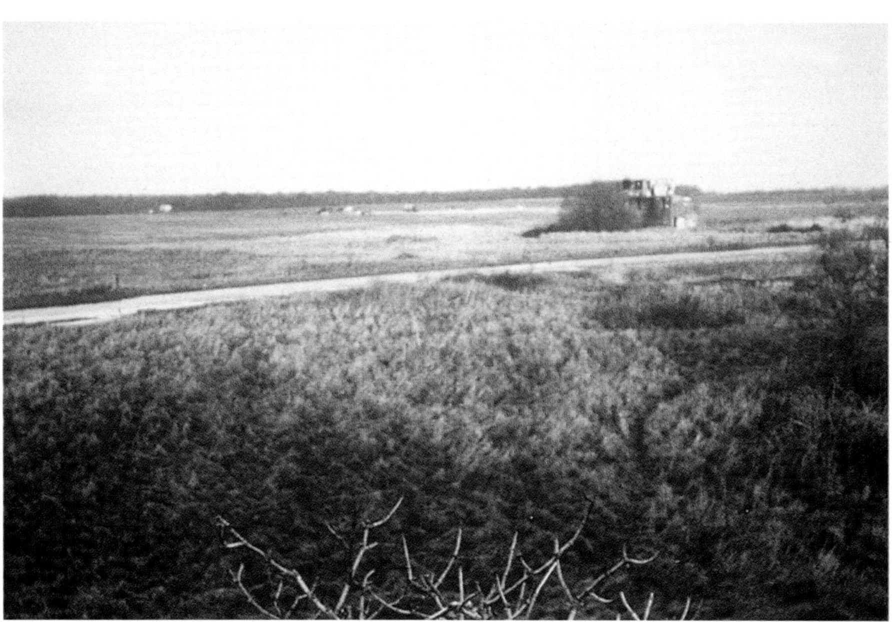

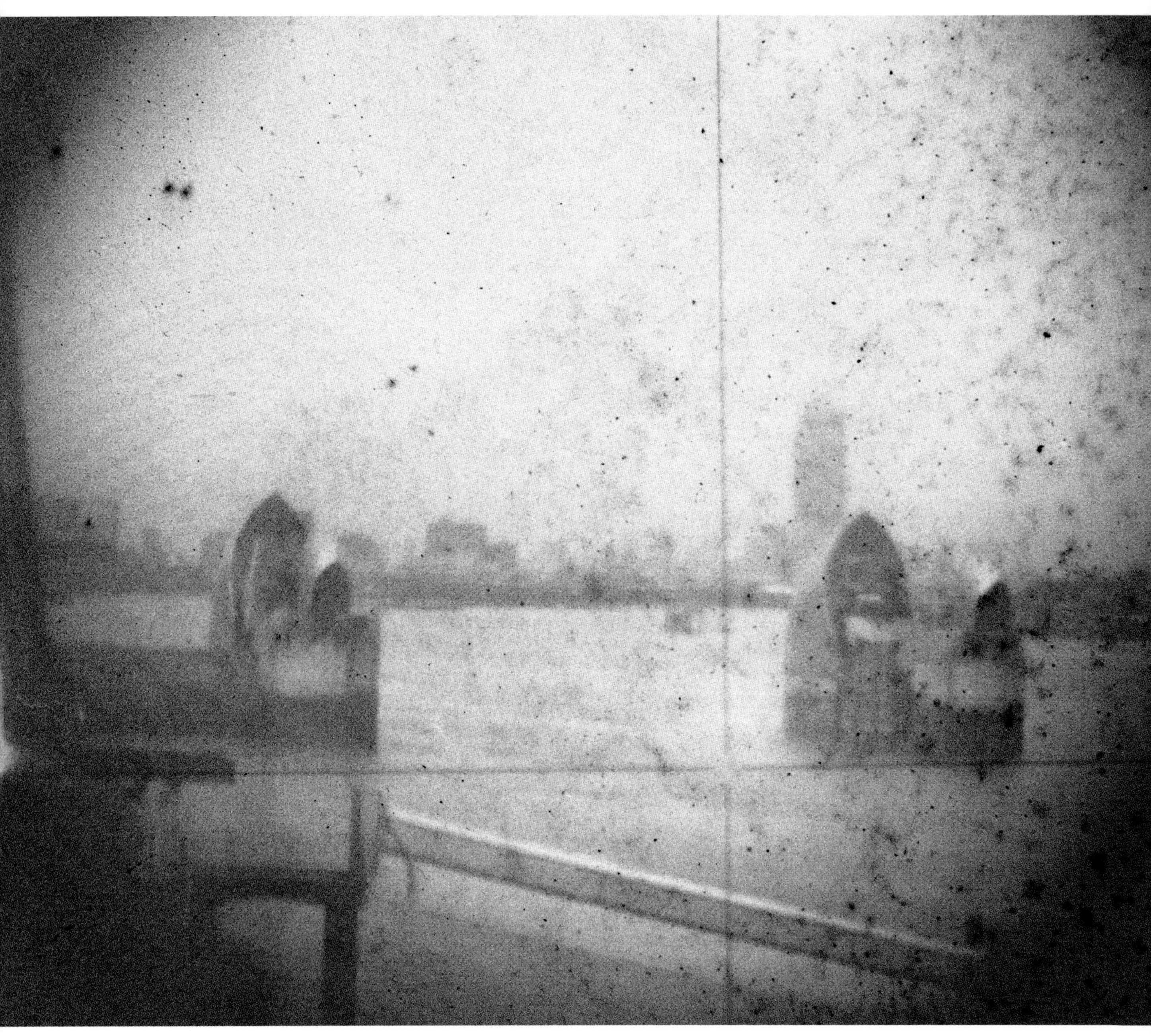

U-475, 1995
Photographs taken through the periscope of a former Soviet submarine moored at Greenwich on the River Thames, London

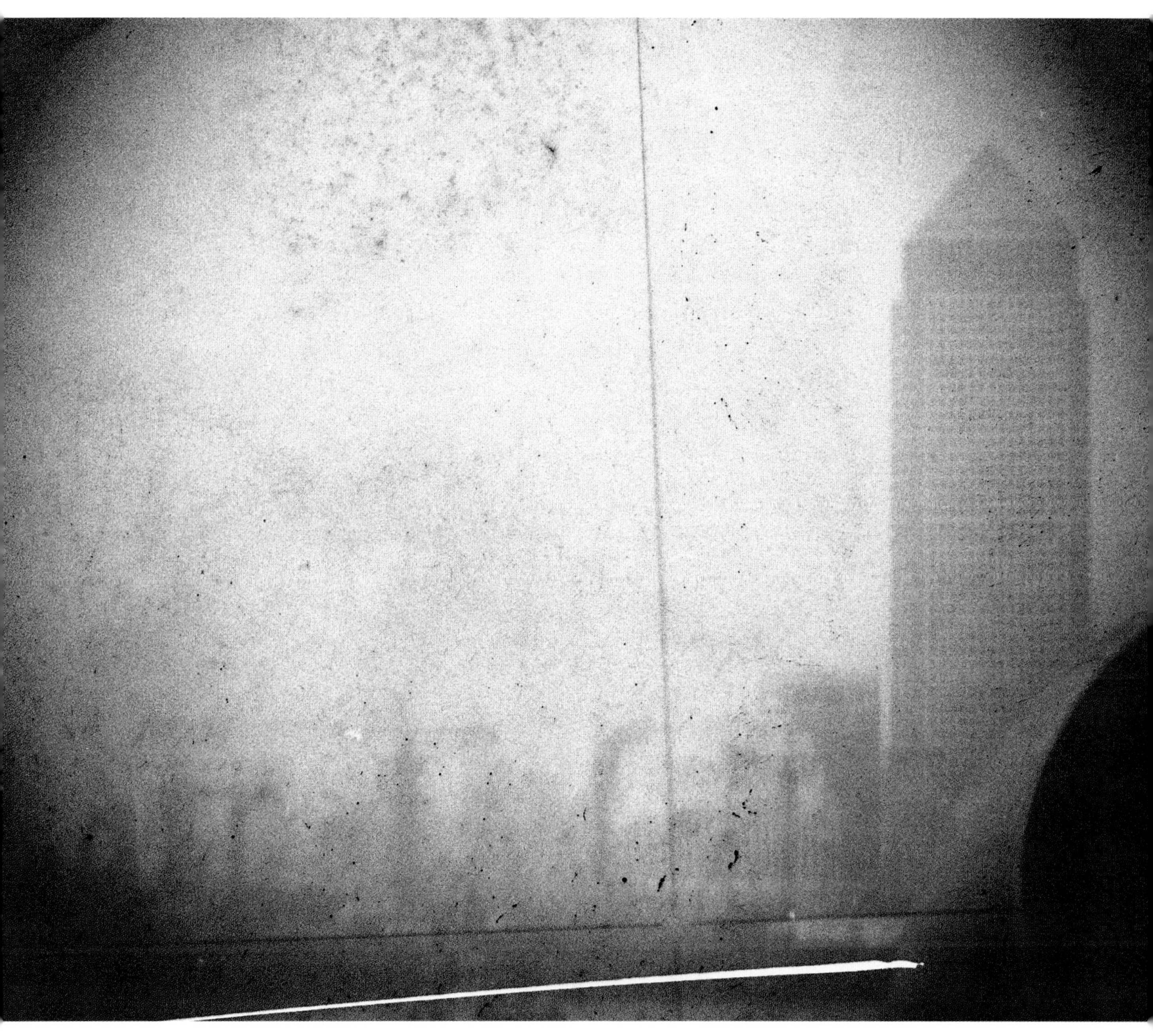

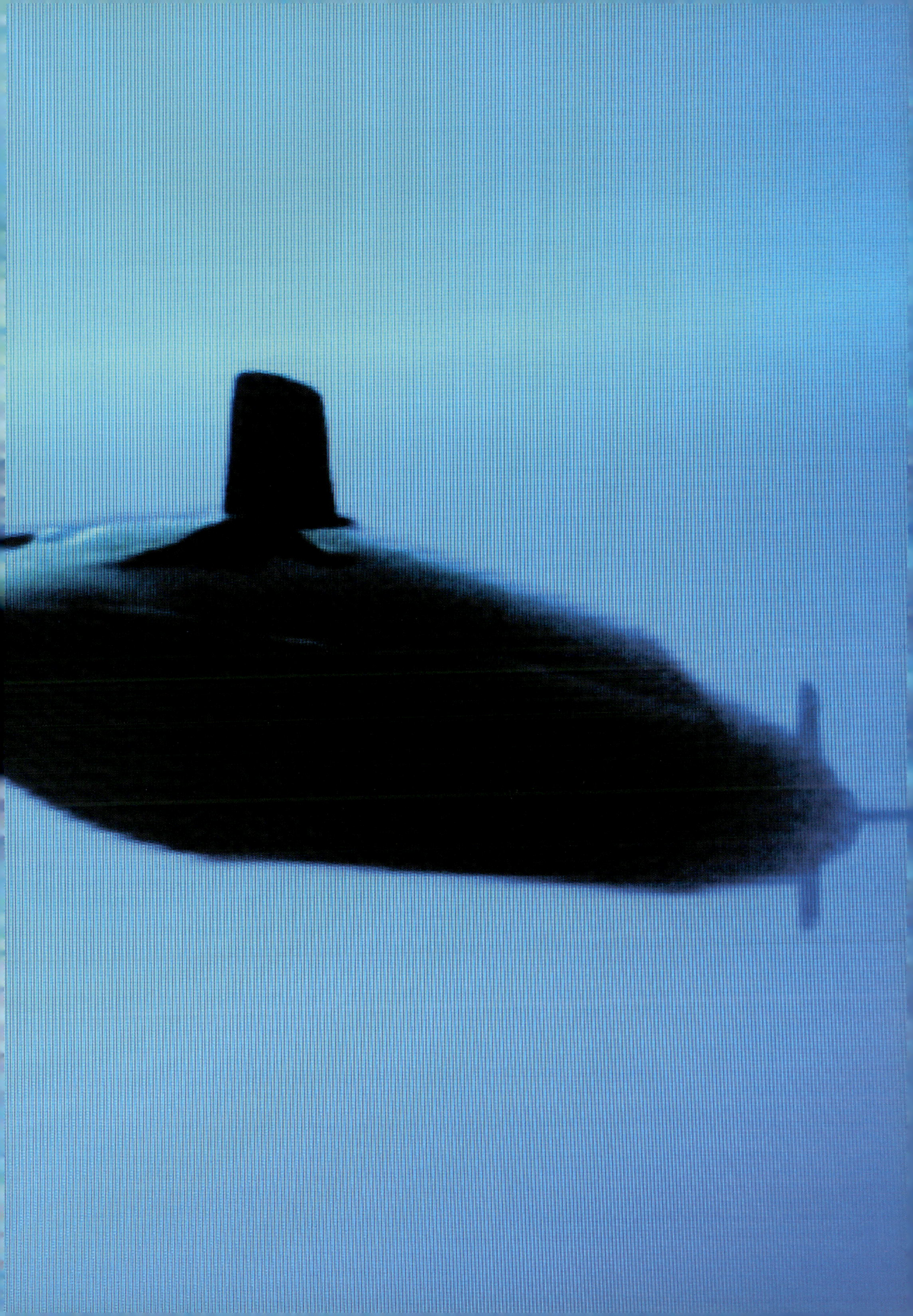

Strategies of the Artist

The artist's imagination is a world of potentialities that no work will succeed in realising.[5]

Artistic practice is slowly finding a place in a world of imagined, as well as real, communities, and Stefan Gec's work contributes to this vital development. The different experiences and biographies of Gec's subjects, collaborators and, indeed, his own biography, means that the monolithic meaning of a word like 'culture' has to be broken down into smaller pieces – made light – in order for it to have any meaning. It is in order to achieve this meaning, in as powerful a way as possible, that Gec has developed particular yet versatile strategies that enable him to work as an artist.

How might an artist develop a practice that acknowledges the radical conditions under which we as modern human beings now exist? Declan McGonagle, former Director of the Irish Museum of Modern Art, tried to answer the question within its historical context by asserting that:

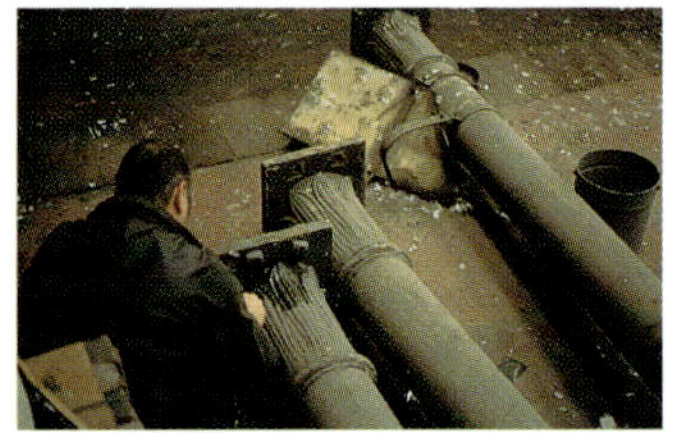

Preparing columns for pattern making, Roundhouse, Derby, 1997

Opposite: *The Ouside World*, 2002

... if the function of the nineteenth century was to fix value, then the function of the late twentieth century model must be to unfix value. Many of the most interesting contemporary artists add the public domain, in the broadest sense, to gallery practice. We can pursue Classical references further and think of the forum in ancient Rome or the agora in ancient Athens as places where social interaction and transactions took place – horizontal rather than vertical distribution of value.[6]

Whether one would want to say that the function of late twentieth century art might also be to relocate as well as unfix value is a matter of choice, yet McGonagle's main point, with reference to "the public domain, in the broadest sense" surely is intended to be encyclopaedic, leaving nothing out. The artist's subject is the world.

It is important to be aware of the research and preparatory behaviour that have become habitual to Gec and is the fundamental basis from which ideas arise for his art. Gec tries to remain perceptive and receptive at all times, putting out feelers and browsing the virtual storm of media imagery and stories, in particular from television documentaries, radio and newspapers. This is an attempt to identify subjects that have power, something with particularity or a distinct poetic resonance. Whether these develop over time into a work or proposal, and how this information is fed into Gec's creative process, is largely governed by intuition, and a hope that the material can be used as a vehicle for something else.

It is the nature of the mass media which Gec draws on as the foundation for much of his research: "It is not only tired, harassed, and dispossessed refugees who cross borders and try to become acculturated in new environments; it is also the whole gigantic system of the mass media that is ubiquitous, slipping by most barriers and settling in nearly everywhere... for the media are not only a fully integrated practical network, but a very efficient mode of articulation knitting the world together."[7]

One example of Gec's fascination for media technologies can be seen in *The Outside World*, 2002. The Emley Moor Mast is situated in Yorkshire between Gec's hometown of Huddersfield and Wakefield (the hometown of Henry Moore) and is the UK's highest free standing concrete structure at 330 metres. It is a listed building dating from the early 1970s, and an icon of Post War communications technology. Gec was very aware of this massive structure in the familiar landscape that he inhabited as a young man. It transmits the five main television channels plus radio stations, digital channels, mobile phone and microwave links across the region. The artist's aim is to use the mast to transmit, via television broadcast signals, an animated computer image of the mast itself – the source material for the animation being architectural plans and drawings.

This work operates not just on the obvious primary level – that modern media technologies are a resource for distributing information world-wide – but on a deeper level of media, as itself, articulating powerful and intrusive systems of knowledge across many different borders.

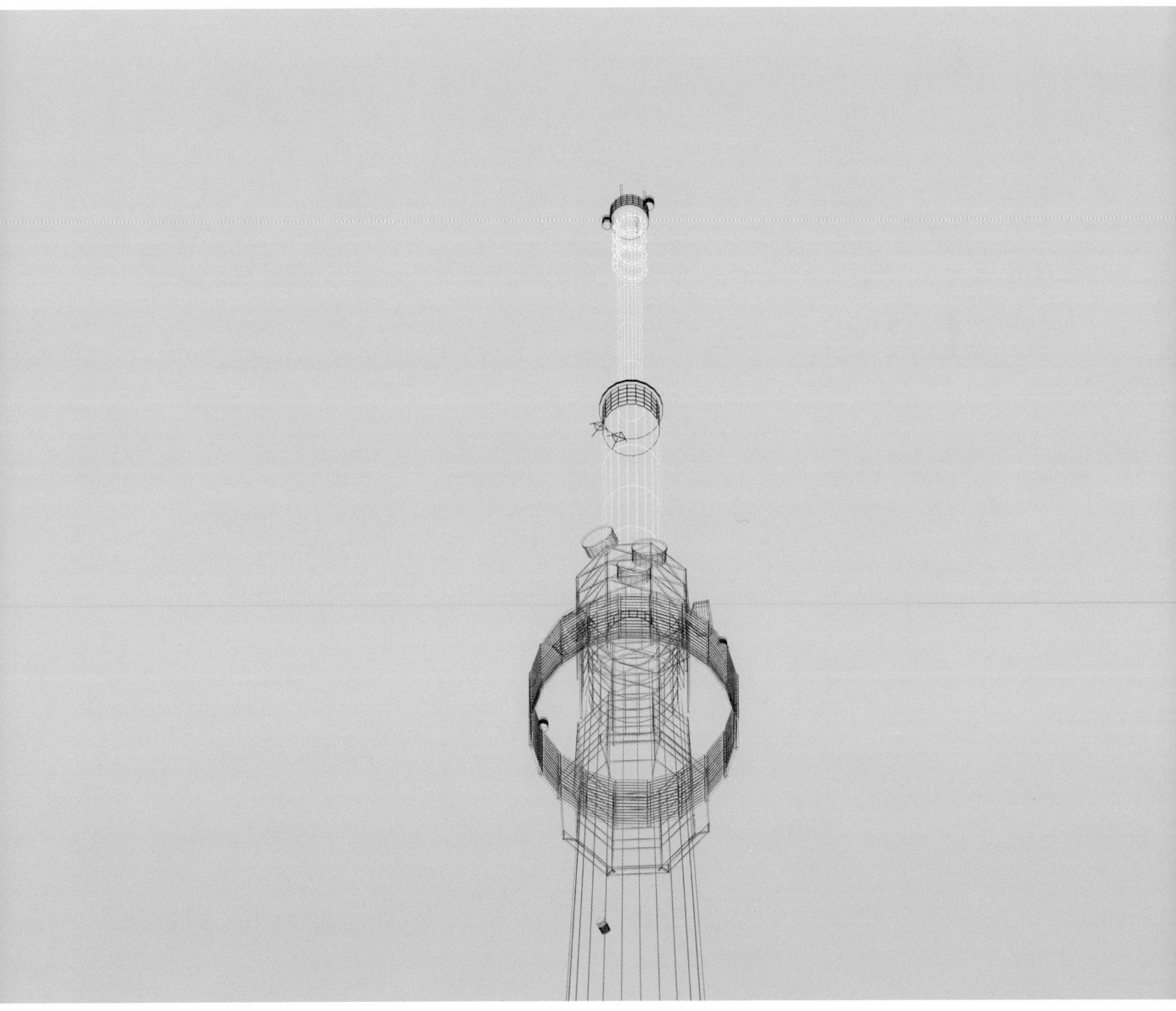

Subjects deriving from traditional or more recent technologies are common in most of Gec's projects. He is an artist who draws on the industrial and technological landscape and our place within it; we are participants, potential victims even, in an industrial sublime. Consequently, the objects and material drawn on by Gec are often familiar, recognisable and clearly belong to the world of work. The artist speculates that at least part of this preference and concentration comes from his experience before training as an artist; working in a textile mill left him with a strong sense of social responsibility and with a view of his artistic vocation that sits uncomfortably with formalism and introspection. The objects he is inspired by or recreates anew – globes, submarines, buoys, iron columns – speak directly of non-artistic and non-gallery-based experience, carry a power invested by another world and have histories that circumnavigate the usual domain of 'art as art'. In an important phrase used by the artist, he "isn't trying to put anything there that isn't there already". The artist as non-interventionist, non-directing, non-interpretative, and deeply aware of the power of his subjects as subjects.

Bloodlines, 1998

Gec is explicit that his work involves an important aspect of memorialising, or what might be termed "marking a moment". A brief analysis of *Bloodlines*, 1998, helps underline this aspect to his art. *Bloodlines* was the response to issues raised by a 200 acre brown field development and regeneration scheme in Derby. Previously the area had been dominated by the railway industry. Three identical pairs of nineteenth century columns recast in iron were placed along a narrow tract of land parallel to a public pathway that follows the River Derwent and marks the edge of prospective building plots. Gec found the original columns, from which he cast his new sets, in the nearby Locomotive Roundhouse – a wonderful relic of nineteenth century industrialisation used to turn engines around but now closed since 1989. (The columns themselves were cast from sections of derelict iron rail track found nearby.) The river, despite its modesty and unobtrusiveness, has been the only constant part of the local landscape over the centuries. One set of columns is near the river edge so they will be covered and uncovered by the changing waterline over the seasons (in a way paralleling the bells of *Trace Elements*, 1990). Gec also produced a 16 mm film, *360°*, 1998, which records the slowly revolving wooden locomotive turntable with a camera positioned underneath its floor. In order to forge connections with the local ex-railway community, and provide another level in which to 'bed' the public artwork, a 'Roundhouse Open Day' was held, where retired or laid-off workers and their families were invited back to revisit and recall their working lives there.

Despite the referential power of *Bloodlines*, it is nevertheless a modest sculptural work, woven unobtrusively into the social fabric of its site. Art, with its colossal history spanning millennia, memorialises the relatively brief history of Western industrialisation, rarely offering support to capitalism and its machinery, only its human subjects. As the artist was very much aware in the making of the piece, even this ostensibly permanent work, in the longer view, is only temporary. All monuments become invisible, either through destruction or over-familiarity. Values do not flow from one age to another and as much as anything Gec's simple motif of paired standing columns seem to suggest that there will always be gulfs in understanding.

Whether we are considering *Bloodlines* or virtually any other of Gec's works, there is invariably the aspiration to mark a position in the world, and give it emphasis. Gec offers the possibility of a deeper response to places and people than would ordinarily be encouraged in our everyday lives. In this regard, the formal simplicity of all Gec's work makes it easier for his audiences to respond as if they are tapping into a wider

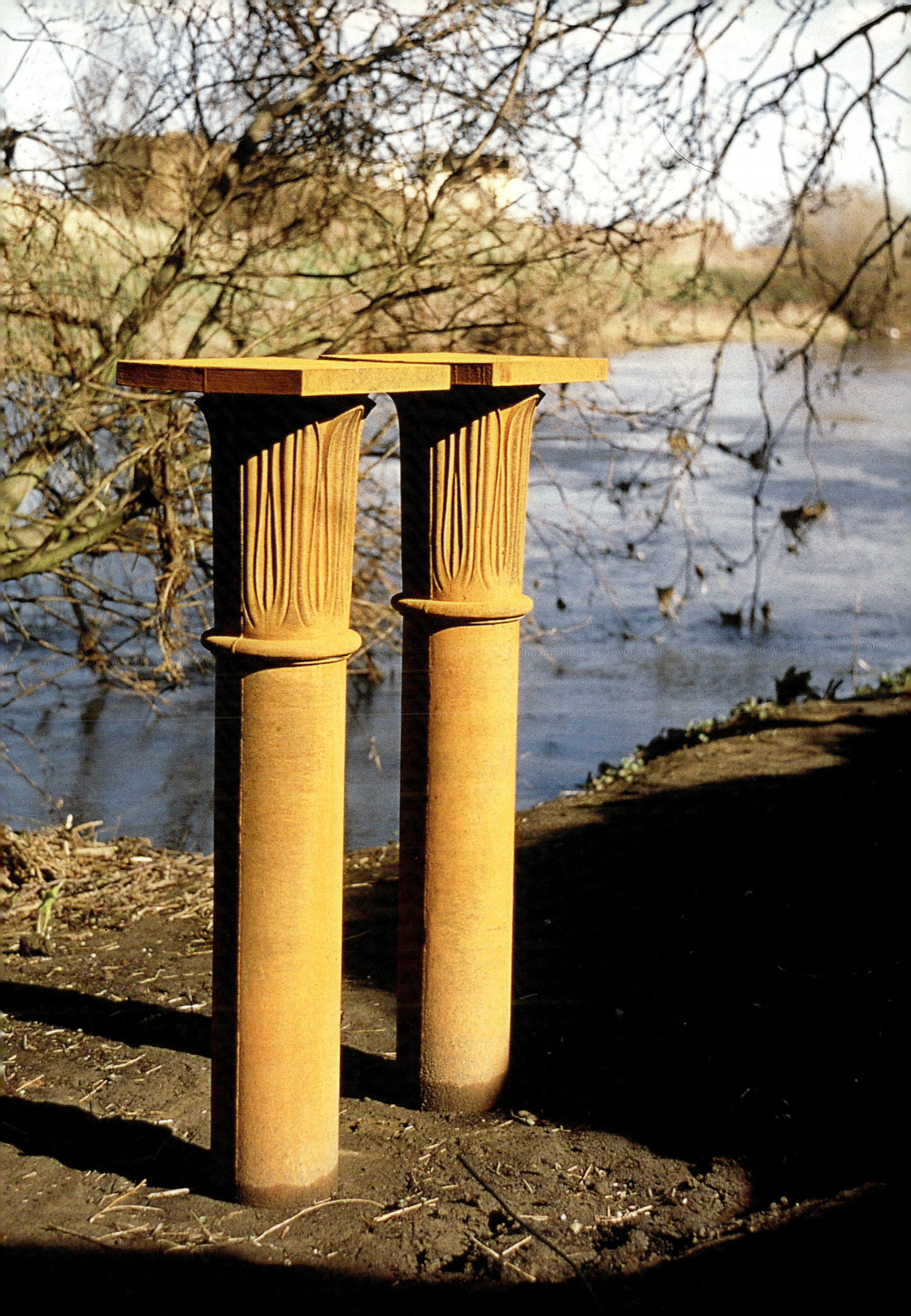

collective memory. For instance, Gec's earlier works that incorporated, literally, the stuff of submarines – *Trace Elements*, *Detached Bell Tower* and *Buoy* – found additional resonance to those familiar with his work in the reports of the disaster around the loss of the Kursk submarine and its Russian crew in August 2000. The skill of combining simplicity and particularity with potential generality is a common aspiration to much art of any century, but one difficult to achieve as successfully as Gec does.

If Gec's art is an ambitious attempt to memorialise and mark a place, it can also be seen then as a strategic move against built-in obsolescence – a common characteristic of much contemporary design in industry and commerce. Gec tries to strip down barriers to obsolescence in order that ideas have as long a life as possible. The works he makes are kept alive, fluid and indeterminate for as long as possible, to the extent that a number of his projects have multiple realisations and reincarnations spanning years, depending on the contexts and commissioning possibilities. It is as if he fears that to create a work that can be grounded and lodged permanently risks the very death of that work, so much so that he has spoken of being primarily interested in ideas that are "everywhere yet nowhere". It is only through constant movement and transformation that Gec's art continues to have a life.

A major element in Gec's working method is the careful filtering of ideas, that in themselves offer numerous developmental options, sub-themes and potential links. The filtering process requires time, above all else, of a length necessary to allow Gec to work through the thinking and rethinking of possible scenarios. Successful ideas are those reduced to a pure essence, honed down in terms of their form and content (particularly apparent in works such as *Fædm*, a simple globe, or the eight bells of *Trace Elements*) but which still carry enough information to enable the audience to draw their own conclusions and make their own connections. In many works such as *Fragment / Vengeance*, 2000, or *Bitter Waters*, 1990, discussed below, the artist seeks something which he describes as "poetry edged with danger". One of the reasons for the careful and deliberate way Gec works up his ideas relates to the modest aspirations in general he has concerning the power and place of art, and the respect he has for the usually 'non-artistic' subjects which inspire him. Compared to the lives of the people who populate the environments he draws on in his work, he believes that art itself offers only a relatively small contribution within the wider public realm. Consequently, Gec is often surprised when his work engenders powerful, positive responses in people who have no training in art.

Eventually, and despite all the processual and background work described above, the artist only intervenes in society when something is made and exhibited. This aspect of making was beautifully encapsulated by the philosopher Hannah Arendt:

Whenever the intellectual worker wishes to manifest his thoughts, he must use his hands and acquire manual skills just like any other worker. In other words, thinking and working are two different activities which never quite coincide; the thinker who wants the world to know the 'content' of his thoughts must first of all stop thinking and remember his thoughts. Remembrance in this, as in all other cases, prepares the intangible and the futile for their eventual materialisation; it is the beginning of the work process, and like the craftsman's consideration of the model which will guide his work, its most immaterial stage. The work itself then always requires some material upon which it will be performed and which through fabrication, the activity of homo faber, will be transformed into a worldly object. The specific work quality of intellectual work is no less due to the 'work of our hands' than any other kind of work.[8]

Finally, and perhaps to bring the pragmatics of the artistic situation to the fore, we must consider the studio as a place of work for the artist. Unusually, Gec has a way of working that is above all a system for moulding and organising ideas; therefore only a computer, a telephone and a desk are his main tools. The studio is not a place for the manipulation of materials, at least in the conventional sense. The artist has suggested that this direction comes in part from his early contact with the North East commissioning organisation Projects UK (now reincarnated as Locus +) whose tools are, likewise, the computer and the telephone. Art is brought to fruition out of a situation that we would more normally associate with office administration. His own sense of what kind of artist he is, is left hanging and he is clearly reluctant to position himself as either a 'public' or a 'gallery-based' artist. Gec aspires to have an art practice that breaks the boundaries art usually moves in – which could mean both the kinds of sites it is positioned in (such as *Buoy*) and in terms of the kinds of audience it has (such as the shipyard community of Barrow in Cumbria). It instead becomes important to keep the processes of making art at least partly enigmatic and open. As a result, the audiences, those who confront and consider the work he does, have virtually complete freedom to draw on his work in whatever way matches their own experience. They are not going to be heavily directed by the artist.

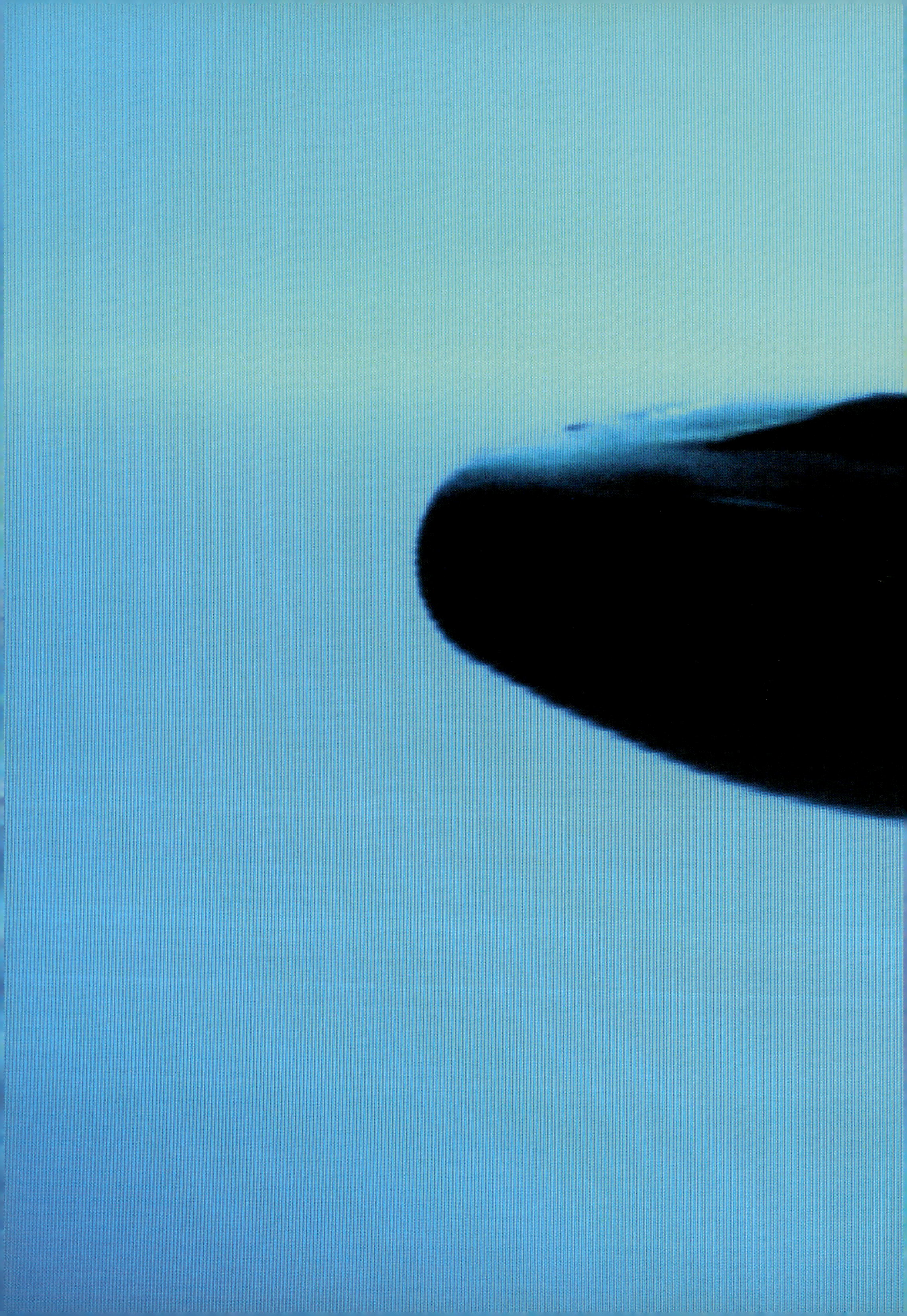

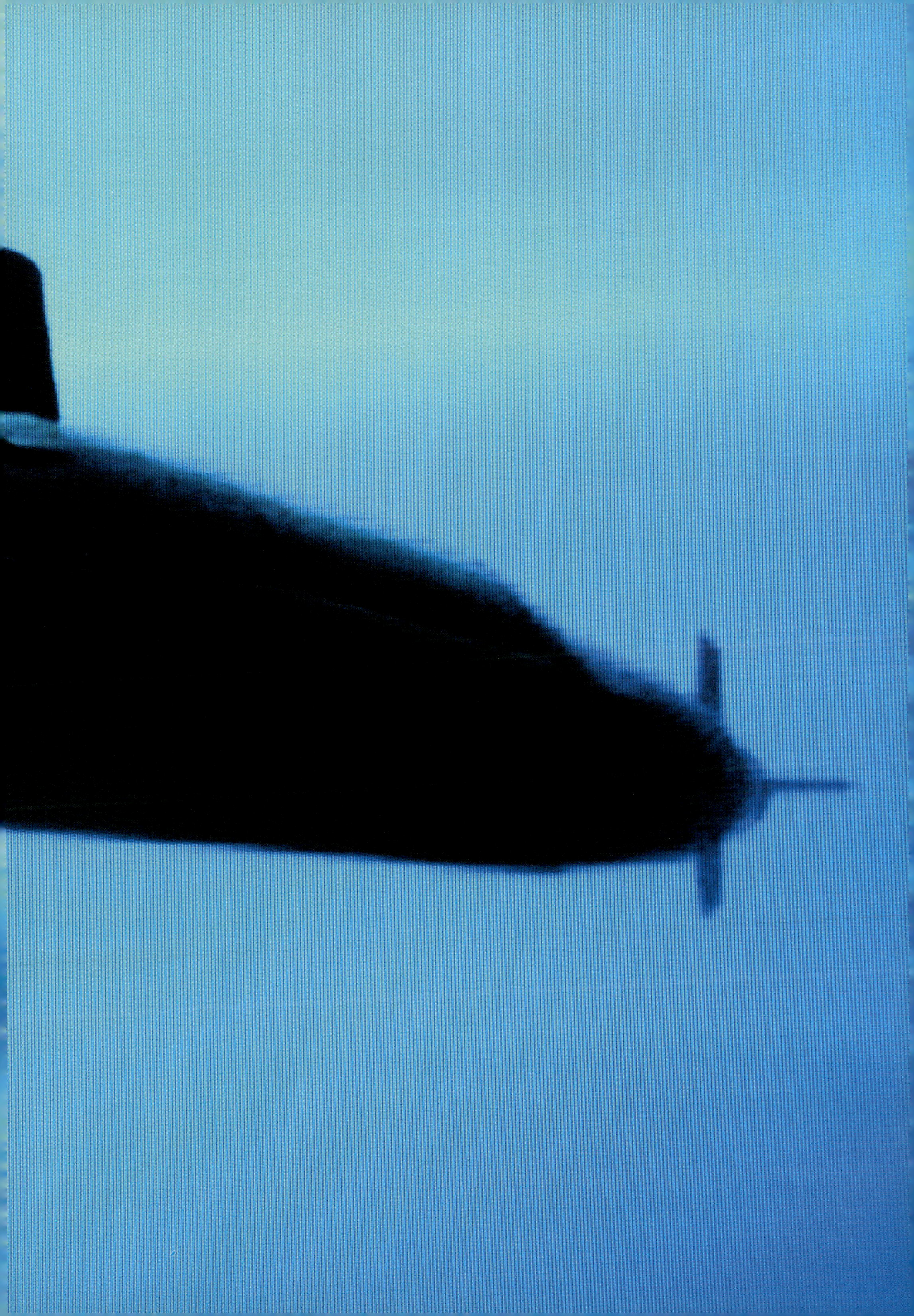

Under Pressure

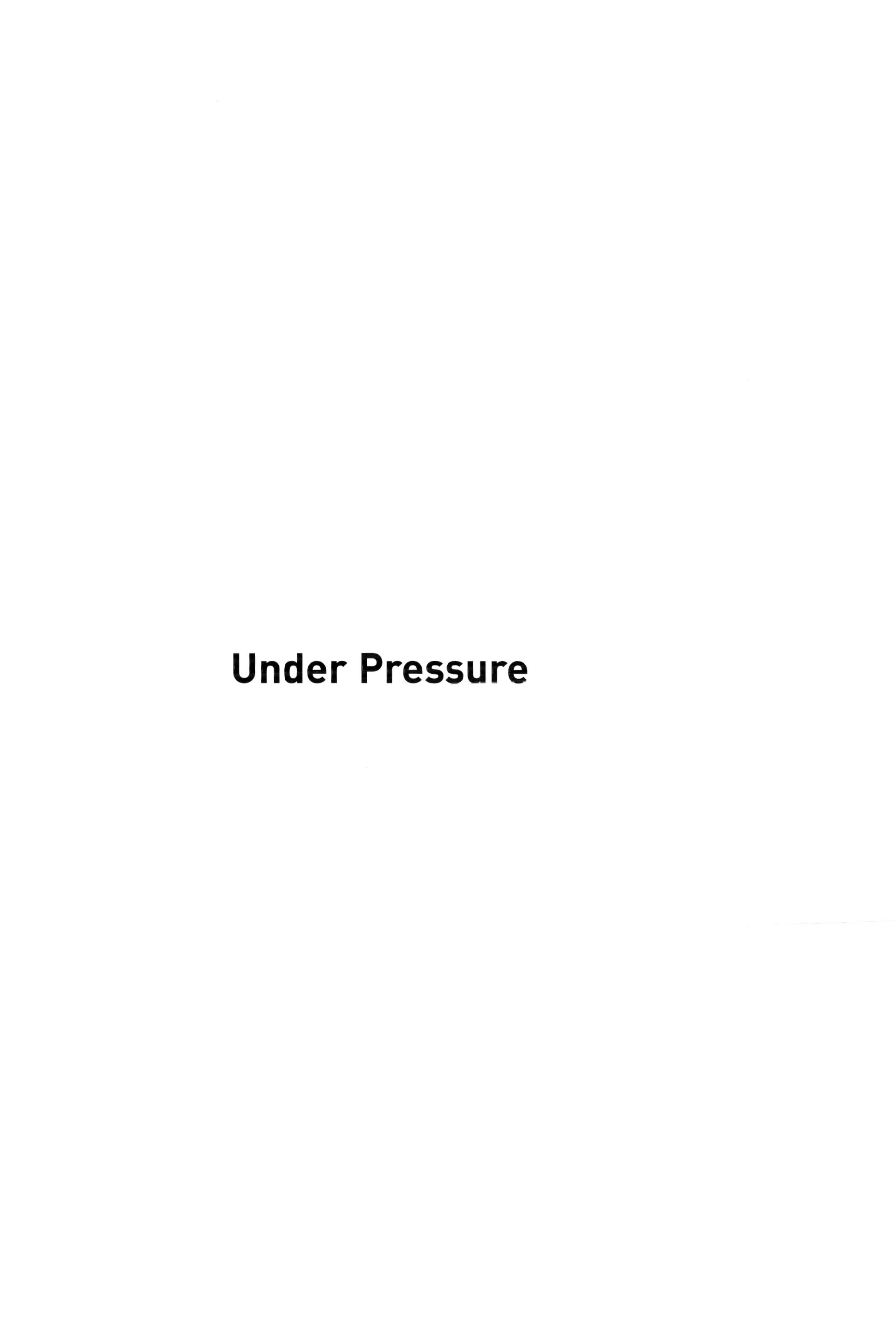

The artist noticed that air bubbles were released from the globe as it was decompressed rapidly back to normal pressure; the equivalent of the bends, when human blood bubbles with nitrogen prematurely released during hurried resurfacing by deep sea divers. The globe, relating back to its register of a human embrace, can to some extent be anthropomorphised, as a surrogate living being exposed to the dead weight of underwater pressure. The origins of the word 'fædm' also include the object of an embrace, which could and did mean a person. It also extended to being a measure of comprehension – what our intellect can grasp – which has come to us as being able to 'fathom' something out. The associated sense of being able to penetrate or see through something offers a link to the artificial clarity with which the *Fragment / Vengeance* animated projection was realised.

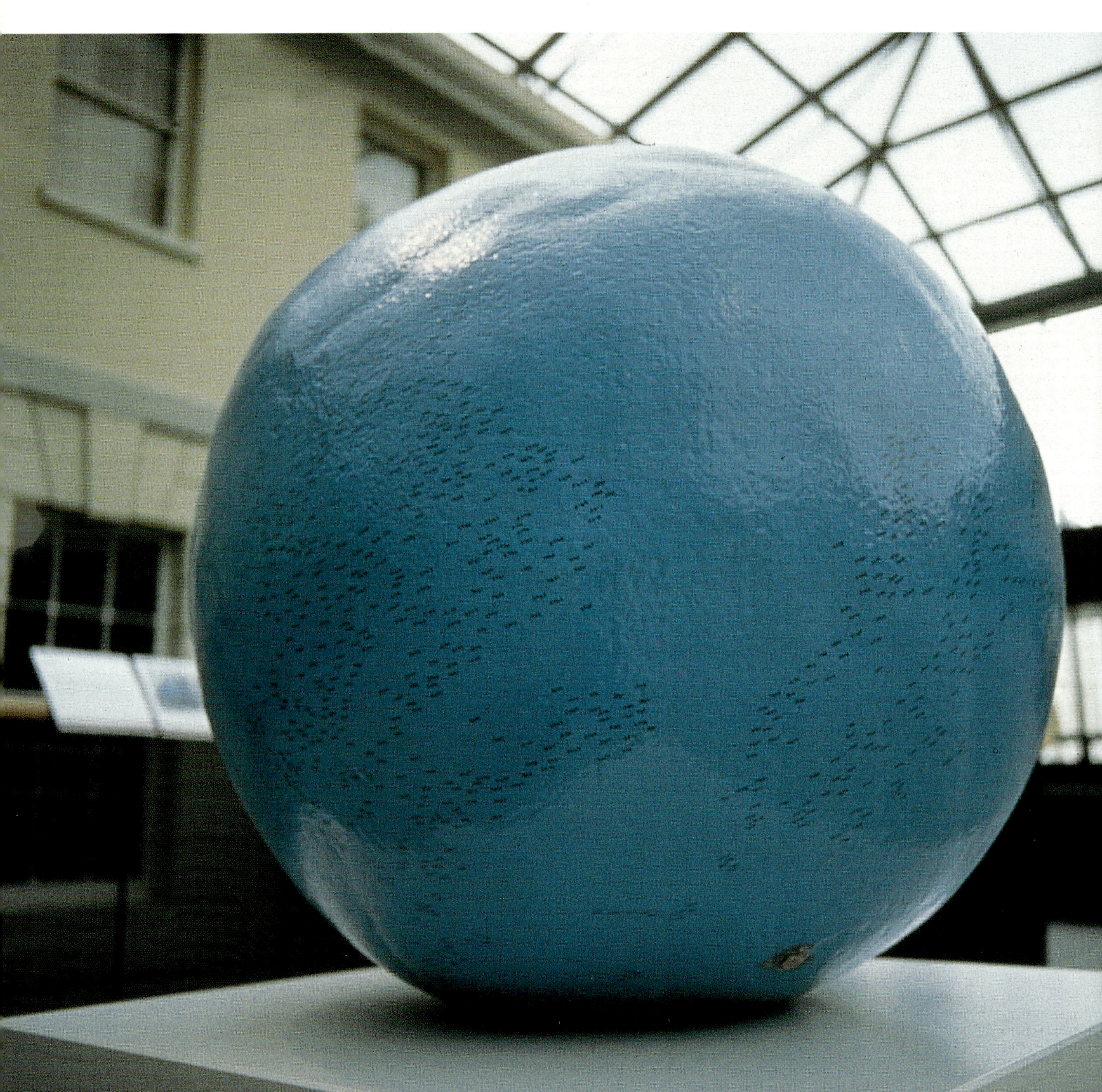

Fædm

Full fathom five thy Father lies

William Shakespeare, *The Tempest*

Fædm was a commission for a new work to mark the opening of the newly refurbished National Maritime Museum in Greenwich, London, as part of an exhibition *New Visions of the Sea*. The term 'fædm' is an old word with two dominant meanings, firstly as an embrace, encircling with extended arms, or secondly as approximately the length of a man's reach from finger tip to finger tip. Over time it has moved into nautical and mining parlance as a unit of depth becoming the more familiar 'fathom'.

Gec looked at the world-renowned globe and map collections of the National Maritime Museum, where a significant amount of the history of western commerce, trade routes, exploration and colonial mapping is contained. He was struck by how powerful a tool globes and maps are in the context of world trading over the centuries, a perception reinforced by the phrase of Le Noury from 1875 which evidences the imperial attitude towards geography: "Geography, that science which inspires such beautiful devotedness and in whose name so many victims have been sacrificed, has become the philosophy of the earth."[9] Gec had a sphere made of painted polyethylene foam, a new globe with a circumference of six feet, approximately a fædm, on the surface of which were as many as one thousand numerical pen transcriptions representing various depths in fathoms around the world. These small three and four digit numbers only registered sea depth and left the land masses as blank. Collaborating with the National Hyperbaric Centre in Aberdeen, the globe was placed in a decompression chamber. The chamber was filled with water and the pressure was gradually increased. The globe was slowly crushed, its surface becoming distorted and creased. The amount of force was finely judged throughout this slow process; the aim being to exert as much pressure as possible without destroying its basic shape and global structure. Heaviness of touch is followed by lightness, which combine to model a form made without touch. The final result is a simulation of the globe going on a deep-sea journey, a passage in time and space, but of course the globe had remained motionless and fixed. It had gone on an imaginary journey into a dimension of the world that was not in the same place as the chamber itself. The judgements that were made about how much pressure to exert introduces an element of performance to the work, the evidence of which traced itself onto the globe's surface.

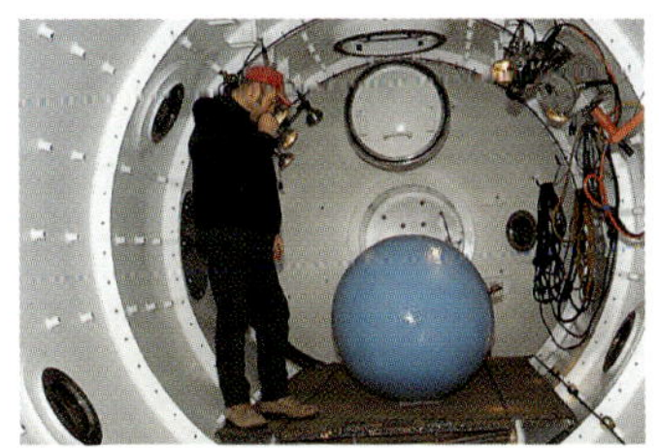

Installing *Fædm* in the decompression chamber, National Hyperbaric Centre, Aberdeen

Opposite: Installation view, polyethylene foam, polyurethane elastomer coating, permanent ink marker

Following pages: *Fædm*, 1999

Fædm articulates Gec's reoccurring concern with "inhospitable environments" (common to other works such as *Fragment / Vengeance*, *Natural History*, *Decompression Chamber*) in which the world is perceived as a dangerous or extreme place where humans find it difficult or impossible to live without protective clothing or specially constructed environments. The globe of *Fædm* is an object on which invisible forces have been exerted but then withdrawn; all we see now are the wounds of this vanished inhospitability.

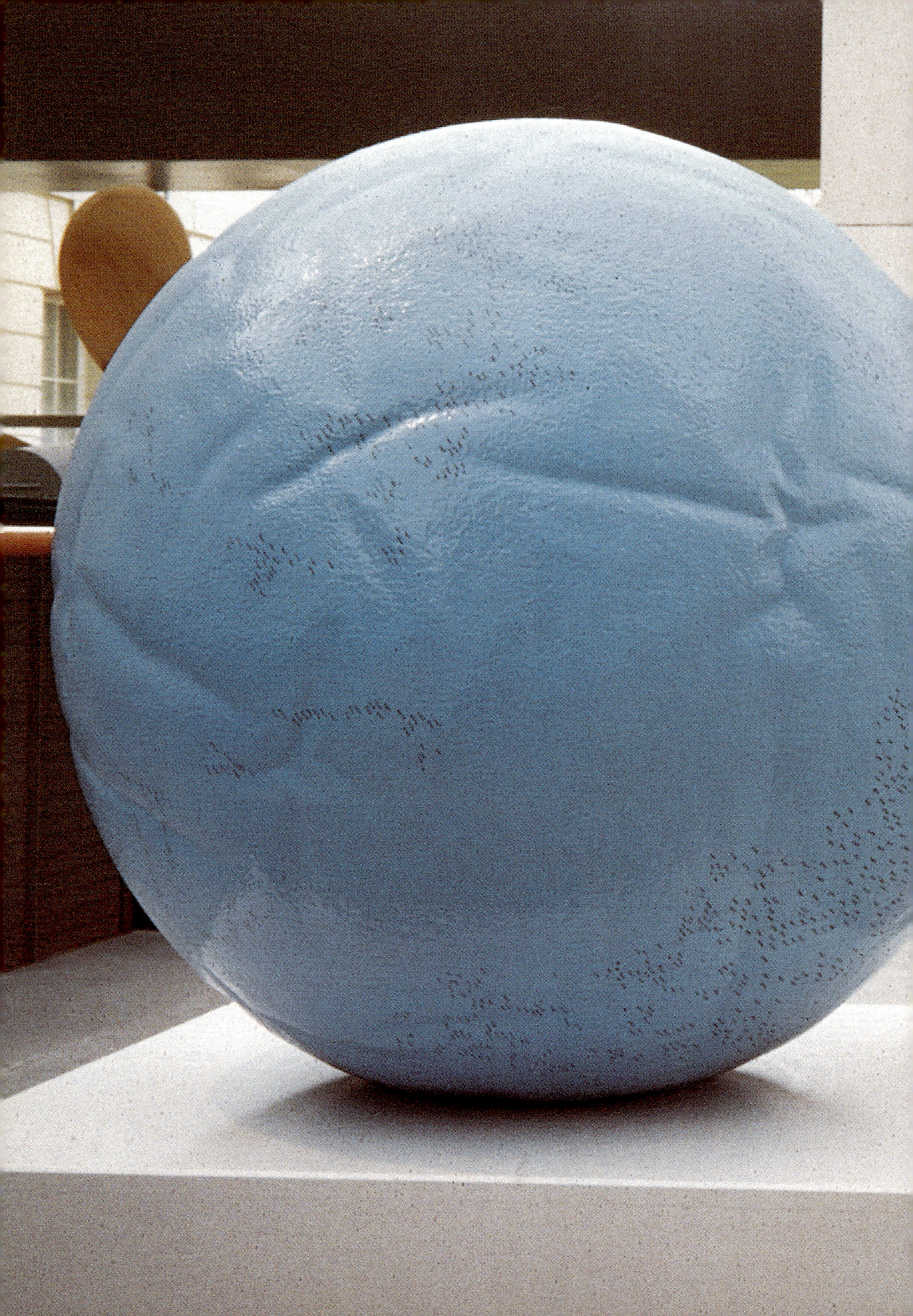

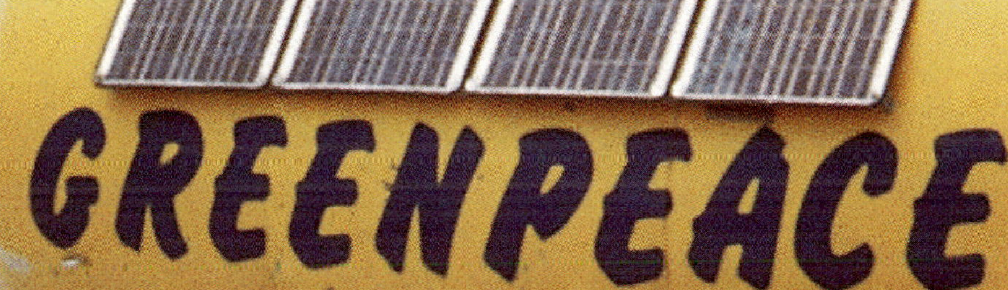
GREENPEACE

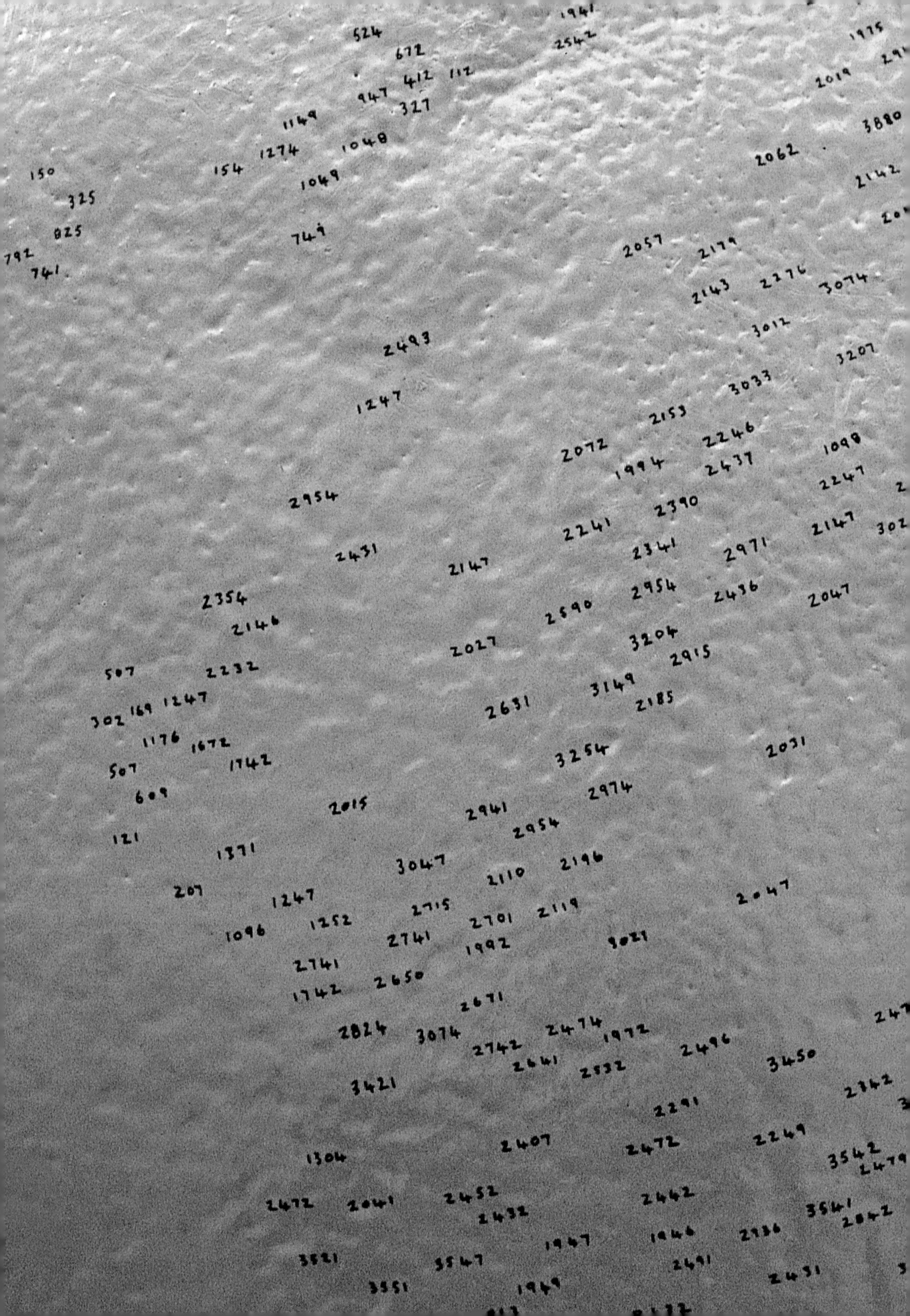

1941
524
2542
1925
672
412
112
947
327
2019
1149
1048
3880
1274
154
150
2062
1049
325
2142
825
749
792
741
2057
2179
2143
2276
3074
3012
2493
3207
3033
1247
2153
2246
2072
1994
2437
1098
2247
2954
2390
2241
2147
2431
2341
2971
2147
2354
2954
2436
2047
2146
2590
3204
2027
507
2232
2915
3149
302
169
1247
2631
2185
1176
1672
507
1742
3254
2031
609
2974
2015
2941
2954
121
1871
3047
2110
2196
207
1247
2047
2715
2701
2119
1096
1252
2741
1992
2741
2650
1742
2671
2824
3074
2474
1972
2742
2641
2532
2496
3450
3421
2342
2291
2407
2472
2249
1304
3542
2472
2041
2452
2442
2432
3541
2042
1947
1446
2936
3521
3547
2491
3551
1949
2431

Fædm, 1999
Detail showing the depths
in fathoms transcribed on to
Fædm's surface

Fragment / Vengeance

Like some heavy thing in deep water

Dante Alighieri, *Paradiso*, III.123

Gec has returned to imagery and processes derived from submarines on numerous occasions. In addition to *Trace Elements* and *Fragment / Vengeance*, discussed below, a less well-known series of photographs (*U-475*, 1995) was taken by Gec of the Thames including the Thames Barrier and Canary Wharf landmarks. The circular images, which have the speckled surface and smoky aura of nineteenth century photography, were made through the periscope of a decommissioned Russian submarine at Greenwich. We see modern monuments to urban and commercial interests memorialised through the optical perspective of an old enemy's now redundant machine. The gap in time between the point at which Soviet submarines were in active use and the series of photographs by the artist is a mere six years, yet he is touching an historic moment that now seems to have all the characteristics of an abyss.

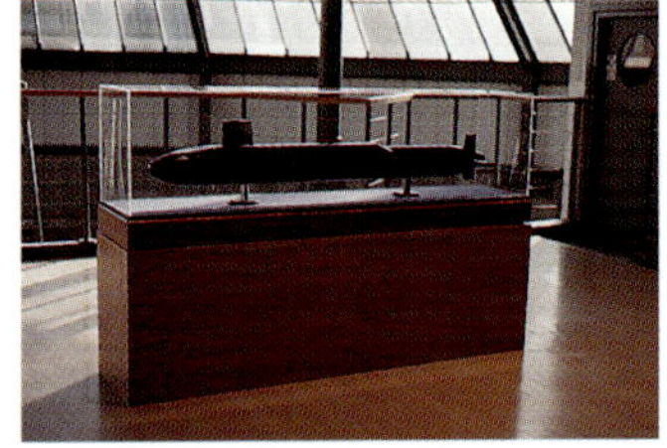

Fragment / Vengeance, 2001
Installation view of Vengeance model, constructed by EDM, Oldham

Opposite: Animation stills

Following pages: Technical drawings for Vengeance (Vanguard Class), supplied by Gerry Hitch, Jecobin

Gec came to Barrow-in-Furness following an invitation from Barrow Borough Council. Barrow is a town which sits on the long, southerly tip of Cumbria, above Lancaster. Its history is that of English industrialisation in miniature – a rise from an eighteenth century farming village to a nineteenth century steel town (based on the iron ore mined around Furness), to finally a twentieth century shipyard town. Following a familiar development that we know well today, namely ethnic hybridity arising from the influx of economic migrants, nineteenth century Barrow was for its time a cosmopolitan mix of Irish, Scots, Welsh, Manx, Cornish and West Indian. Gec's work thrives on the kind of trans-culturalist context that Barrow typifies and it is easy to see why the invitation greatly intrigued the artist.

The economic growth of Barrow over the last hundred years was secured when engineering firm Vickers Brothers moved into shipbuilding at Barrow at the end of the nineteenth century, at a time when naval rearmament swept Europe. Vickers won contracts throughout the century from countries as far flung as Japan, Russia, Brazil and China – all of which concerned the British Admiralty with its eye on British security. Barrow-in-Furness boomed.

The town soon developed an international reputation for building submarines and as a consequence a highly skilled workforce arose over the years. The commission for a major artwork was initiated to coincide with the Barrow Submariners Centennial in May 2001, the 100th anniversary of the first submarine to the built in the town (Holland No.1). In the 1960s Barrow moved towards building nuclear submarines, starting with Dreadnought, launched in 1960. Polaris was followed by Trident in the mid-1980s – the last class to be built (commissioned when there was still a perceived nuclear threat from the Soviet Union). With changes in international 'blocs' and the break up of the East-West Cold War the continuation of submarine building in the area is under review. The Vengeance (Vanguard class) was the last Trident submarine to leave Barrow's shipyard and was launched in late 1998.

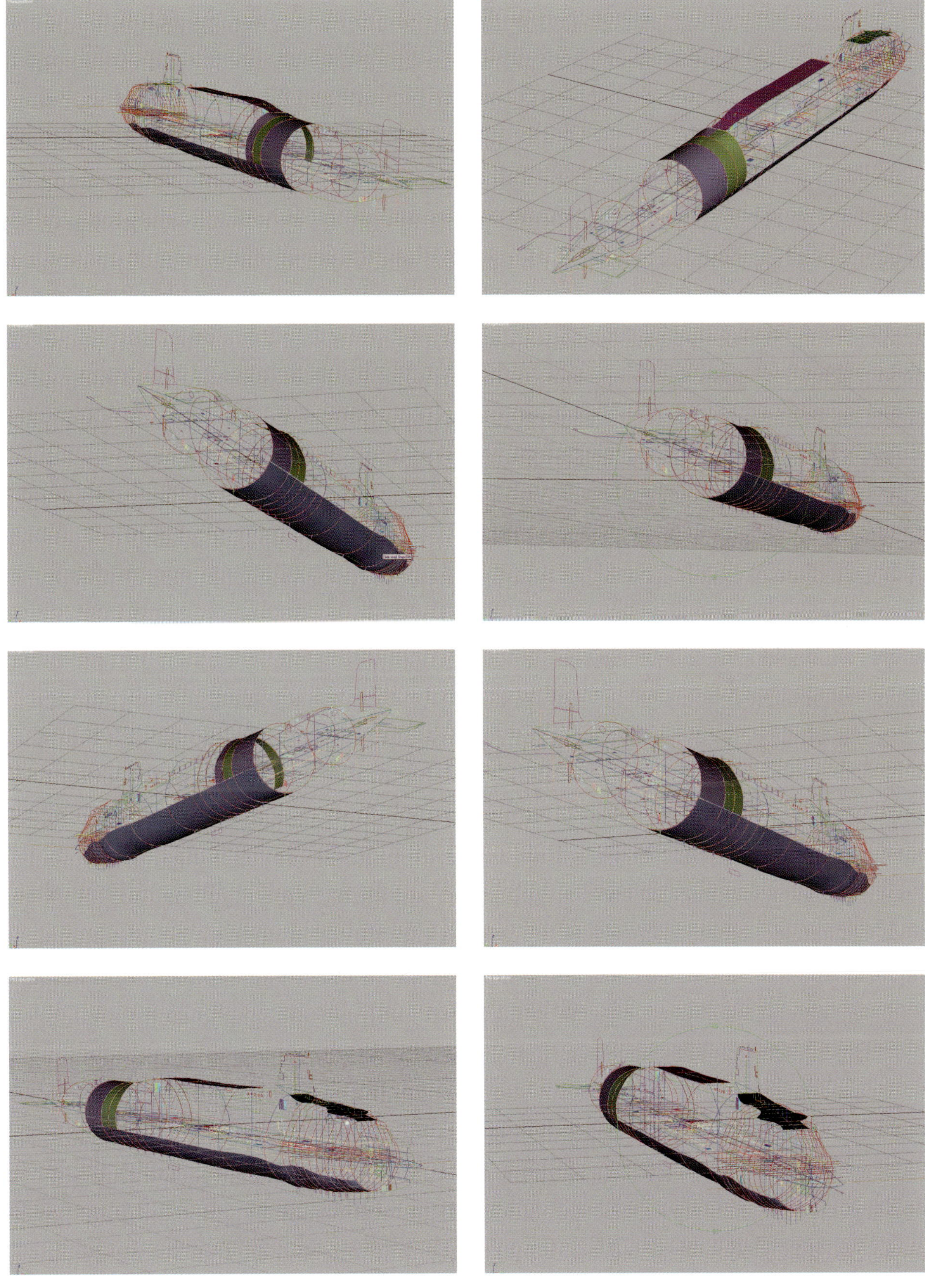

96 1-2

H.M.S. VANGUARD 1998 SSBN S28

SHEET 1 OF 2 | 1:96 SCALE (c) 1999 G.L.Y. HITCH

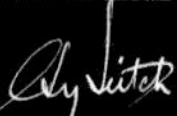

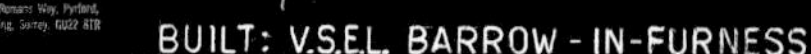

BUILT: V.S.E.L. BARROW-IN-FURNESS.

LAUNCHED: MARCH 1992, COMMISSIONED: AUGUST 1993.

LENGTH: 150M, BEAM: 13·2 M, DRAUGHT: 12 M DEEP.

DISPLACEMENT: 16000 TONNES, DIVED.

POWER: R.R. PRESSURISED WATER REACTOR, 2 G.E.C. TURBINES, 27500 SHP.
PUMPJET PROPULSOR, ONE EMERGENCY PROPULSION UNIT "EGGBEATER

SPEED: 25 KNOTS, DIVED.

CREW: 14 OFFICERS, 121 RATINGS.

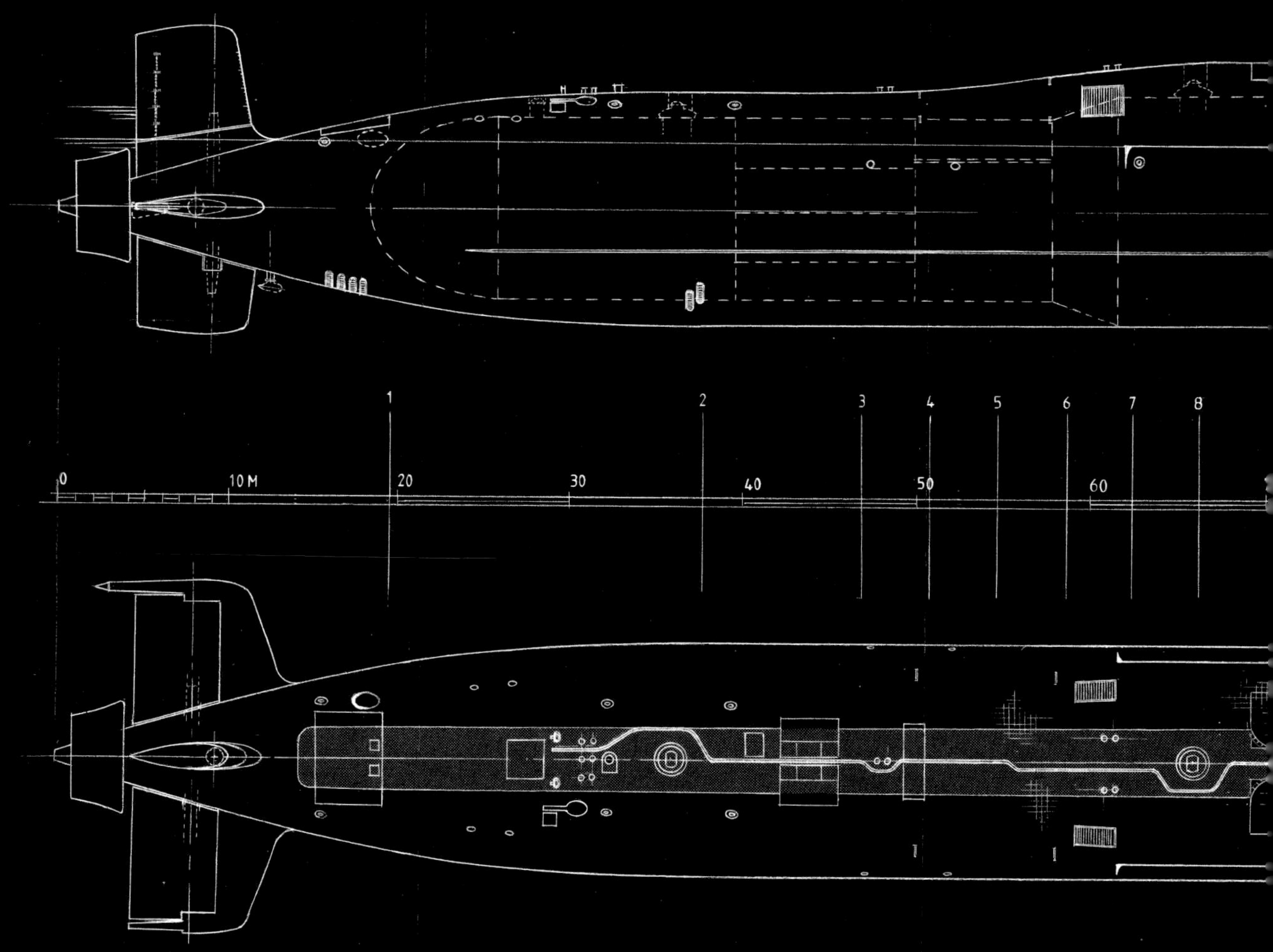

1 2 3 4 5 6 7 8

0 10 M 20 30 40 50 60

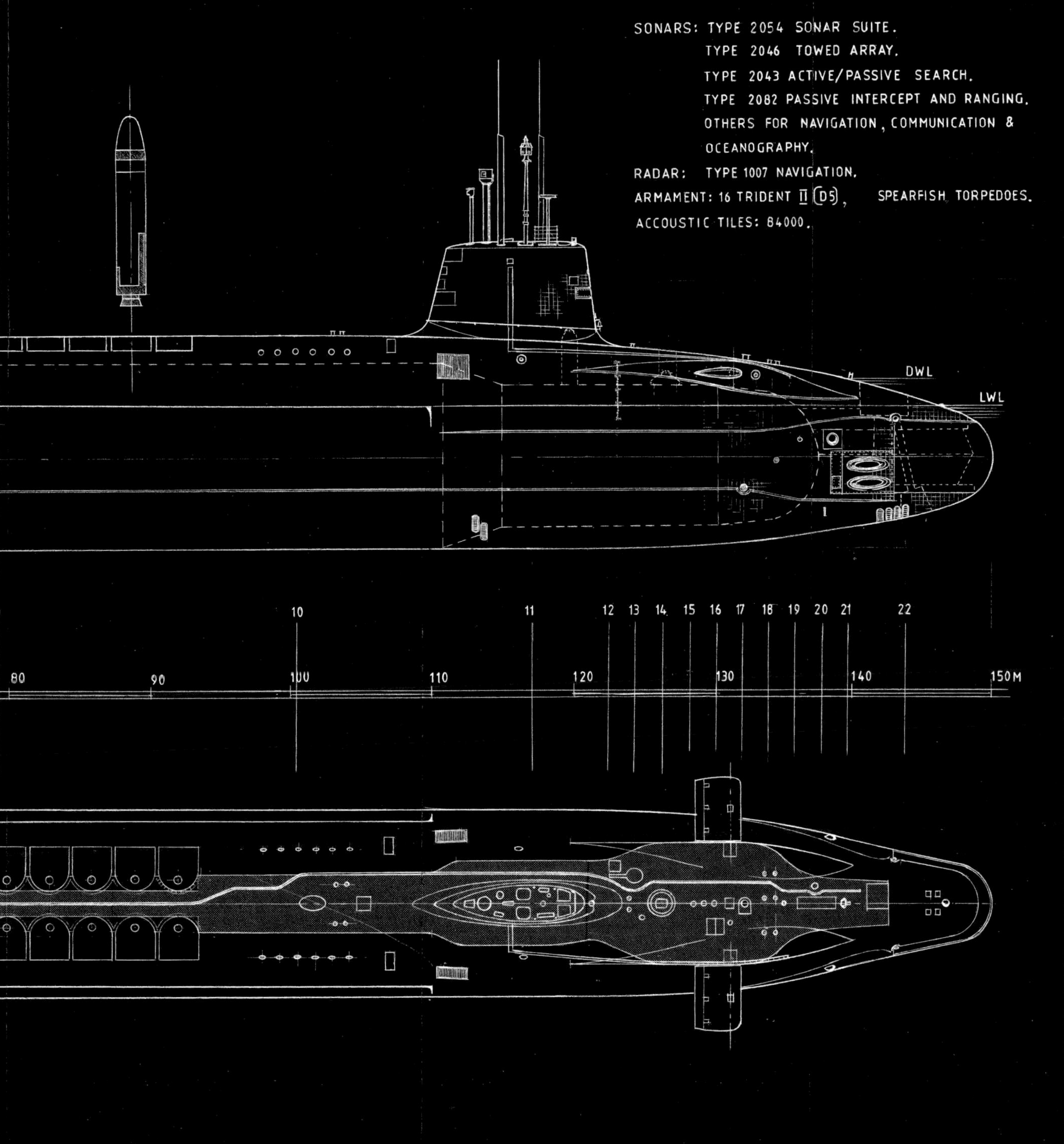
SONARS: TYPE 2054 SONAR SUITE.
TYPE 2046 TOWED ARRAY.
TYPE 2043 ACTIVE/PASSIVE SEARCH.
TYPE 2082 PASSIVE INTERCEPT AND RANGING.
OTHERS FOR NAVIGATION, COMMUNICATION & OCEANOGRAPHY.
RADAR: TYPE 1007 NAVIGATION.
ARMAMENT: 16 TRIDENT II (D5), SPEARFISH TORPEDOES.
ACCOUSTIC TILES: 84000.
DWL
LWL
10 11 12 13 14 15 16 17 18 19 20 21 22
80 90 100 110 120 130 140 150M

Aluminium disk inserted into the model of Vengeance

Installation view of the model

The work force suffered a drastic reduction in the early 90s. By 1998 it had stabilised albeit at a reduced capacity.

Fragment / **Vengeance** is a two-part work, presented in Barrow town centre between 4 and 11 May 2001. The first part consists of a six foot scale model of the submarine, based on Vengeance. The second part took the form of an outdoor projected animation of the same vessel. Both involved the artist researching Barrow's submarine building history. *Fragment /* **Vengeance** is deeply rooted in working experiences of the submarine industry, achieved on an ambitious scale.

The first part of the project might be considered to be the model based on the Vengeance. The production and maintenance of submarines takes place within Build Halls that are huge, purpose-built, secure sheds. The rest of the town's population is shielded from the work that goes on within. From a national security point of view this necessary, enforced pattern is in striking contrast to the usual open relationship between civil shipyards and the surrounding town where shared ownership is more boldly stated. The technical drawings for Vengeance are classified under the Official Secrets Act until 2026, so the look of both the model and the animated projection have had to reference publicly available photographs to estimate the true dimensions of the Vengeance. However, as the model makers EDM Ltd., Oldham, had made models of earlier Trident submarines they could draw on archived plans. In all aspects, including its case decorations and fittings, the model follows the standard Vickers specification extremely closely.

The model which is housed in its own presentation case, has inserted into its hull, flush with the upper surface, a small disk of aluminium taken from a discarded cooking utensil, which the artist found among domestic scrap in the town, linking the model and the domestic world of the workers. Gec was intrigued by the proliferation of amateur model making groups in Barrow particularly among the workers at Vickers who spent their time constructing real submarines during the working week, then building all kinds of models of similar vessels in their recreational time.

The model helps draw our attention to the submarine itself, as an object, which can be seen as a sophisticated example of underwater architecture for living and warfare. The submariners have to live and work very close to the torpedoes, and Gec was struck by the close proximity of the living quarters to the storage of these lethal weapons. He also noticed, with both the highly finished model and the computer-generated rendition, the dramatic contrast of the general appearance of submarines, irregular and human, with pipes and hatches interrupting their seemingly sleek surface.

Which leads us to the second and considerably larger element of *Fragment /* **Vengeance** – the public projection. This consisted of a computer-generated animation video of the Vengeance travelling underwater in a right to left direction. As with the model, the construction of the virtual model for projection had to be intuited from drawings based on photographs, with a line drawing in three dimensions being clad and animated. In May 2001 the four minute continuous video loop was projected on the first night on the exterior of Wilkinsons in the town centre for its first showing, then over the following three consecutive nights on the exterior wall of BAE Systems' Devonshire Dock Hall. The docks' video projection, at 80 x 35 metres is the largest accomplished in the UK to date.

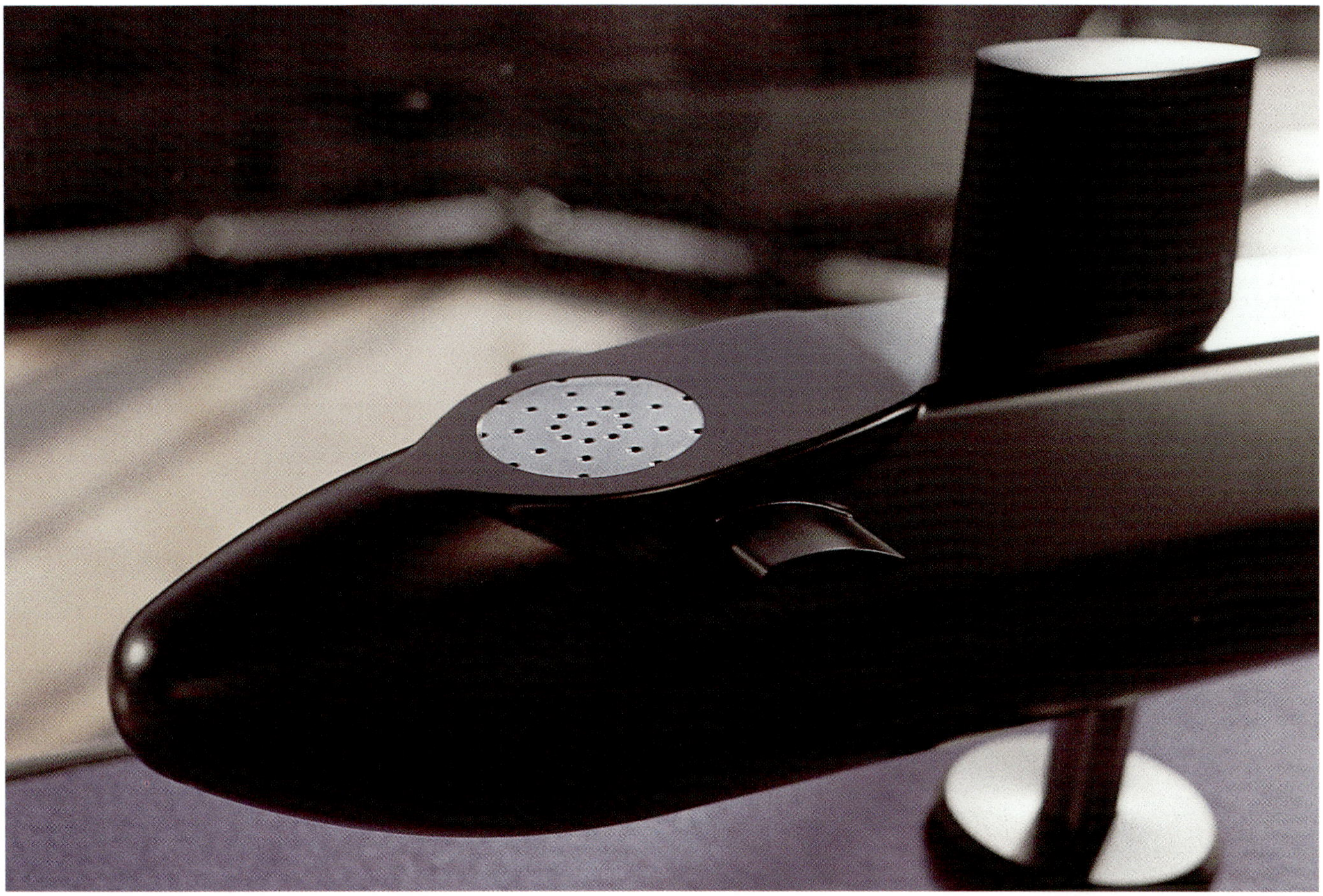

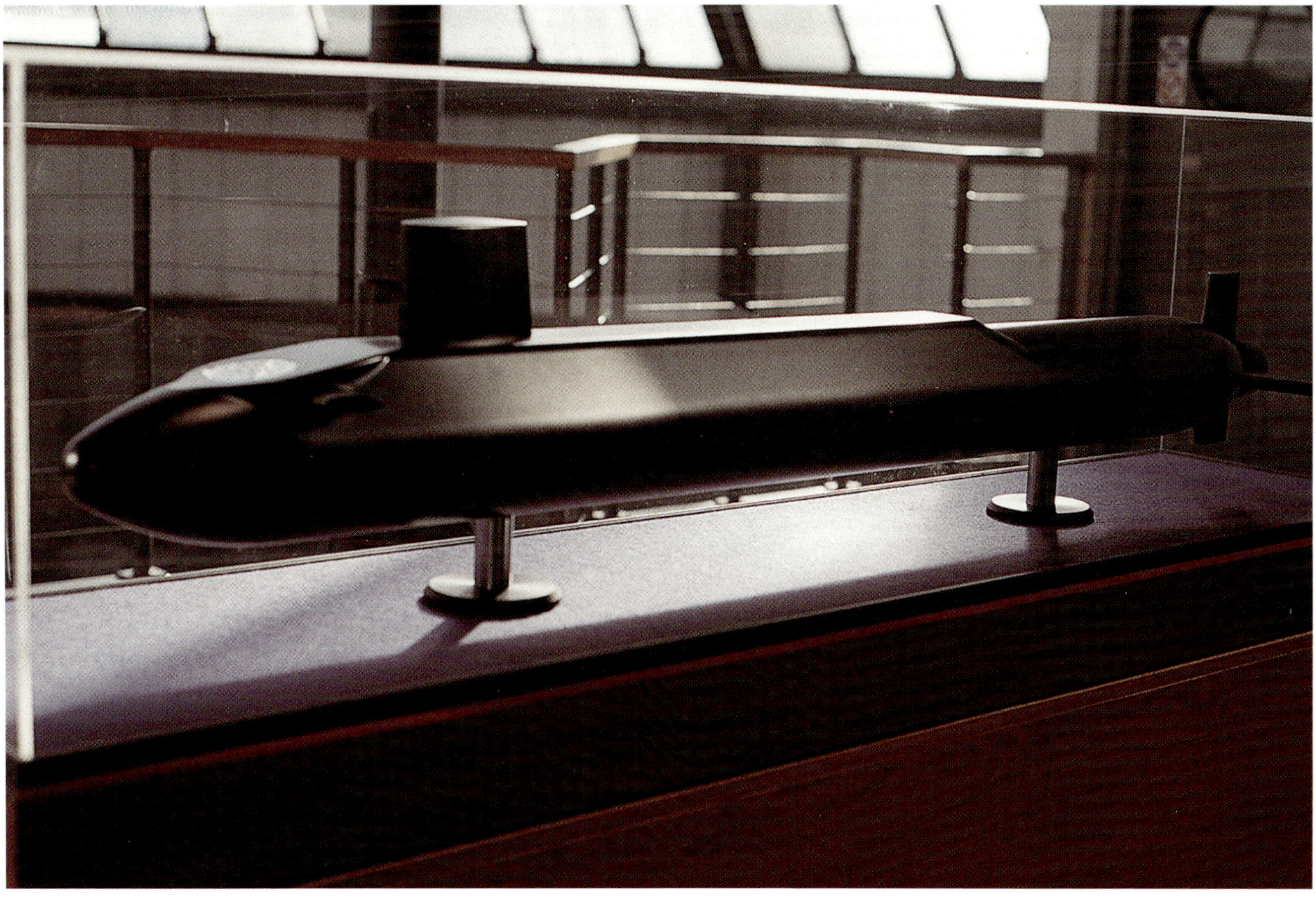

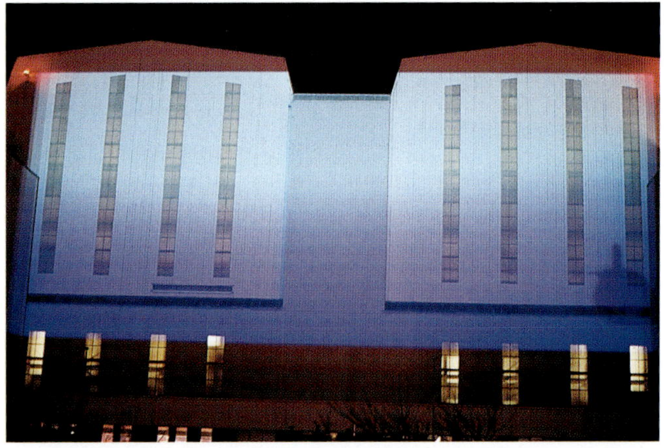
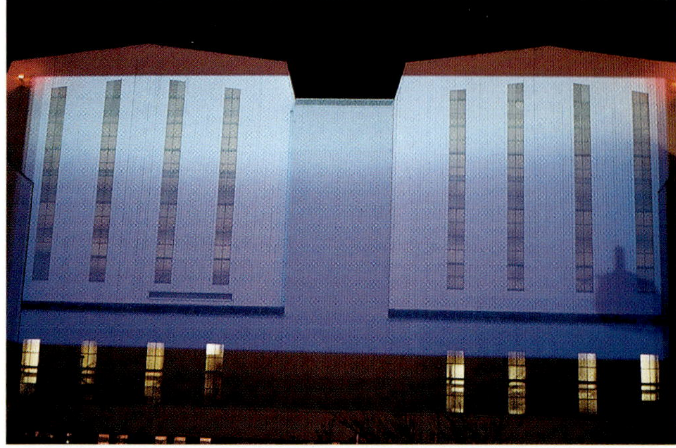
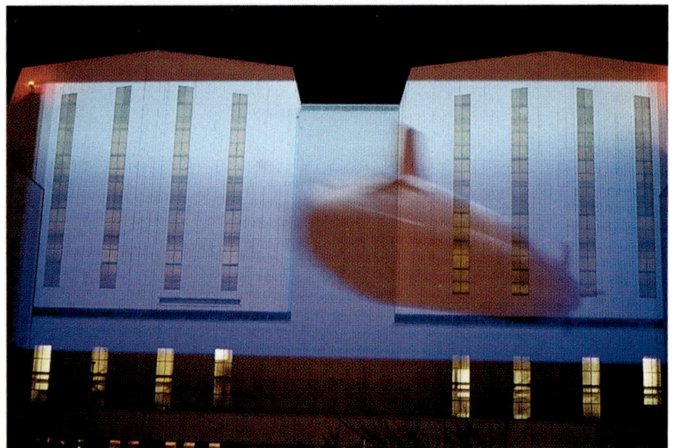
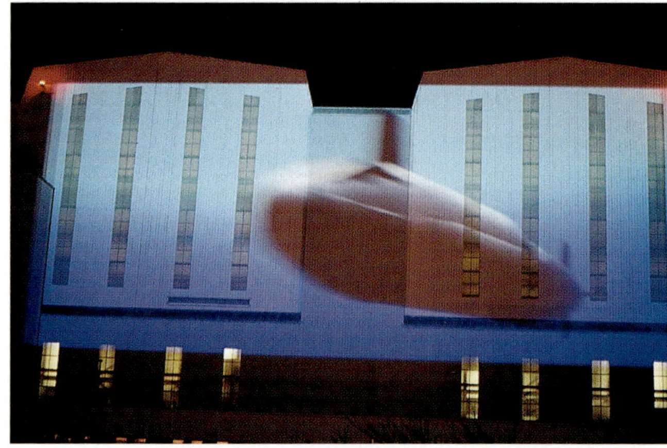
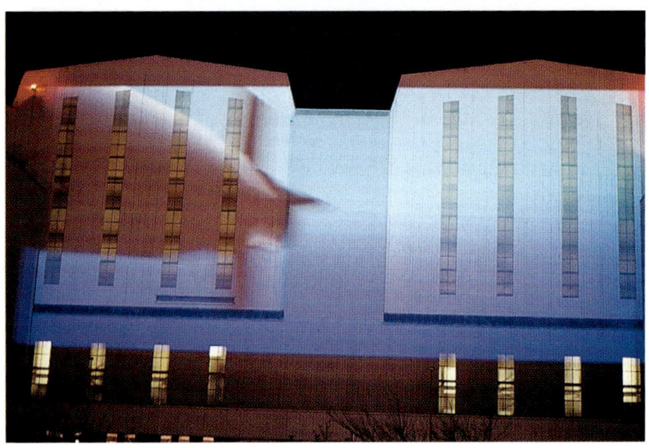
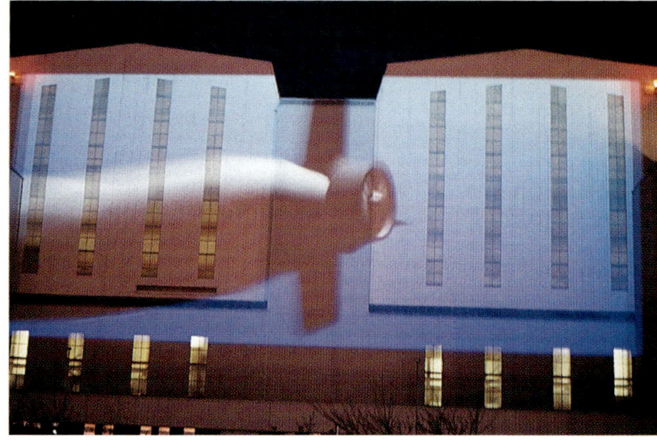

Animation stills,
Devonshire Hall, BAE Systems

Following pages: Installation view of the projection, with Barrow-in-Furness in foreground
Courtesy N.W. Evening Mail

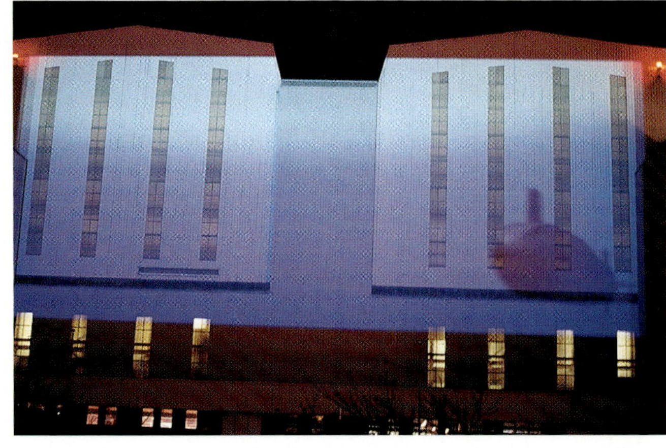
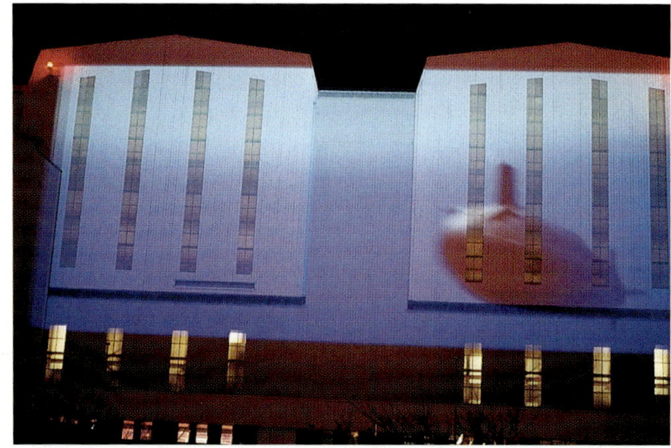
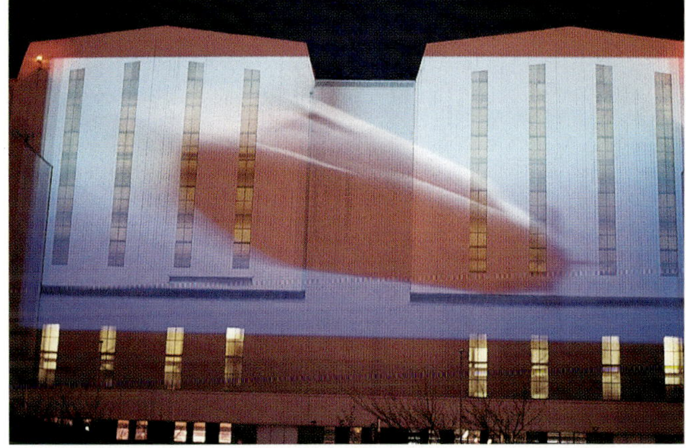
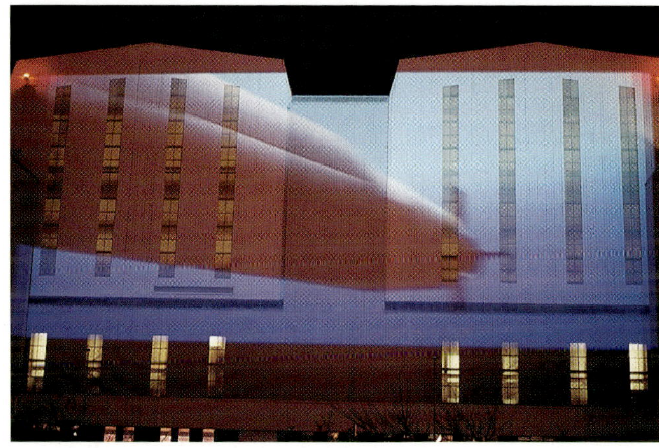
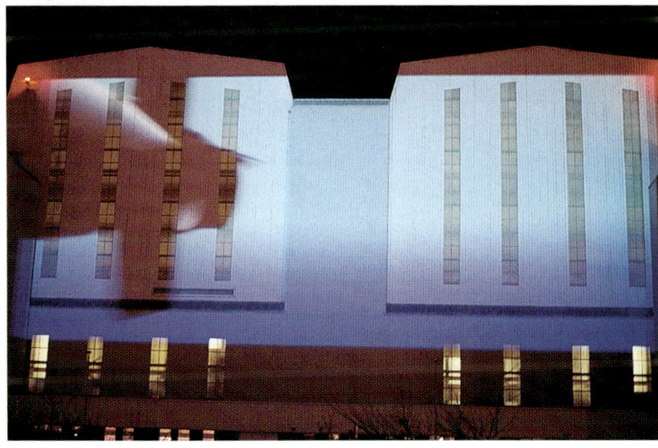
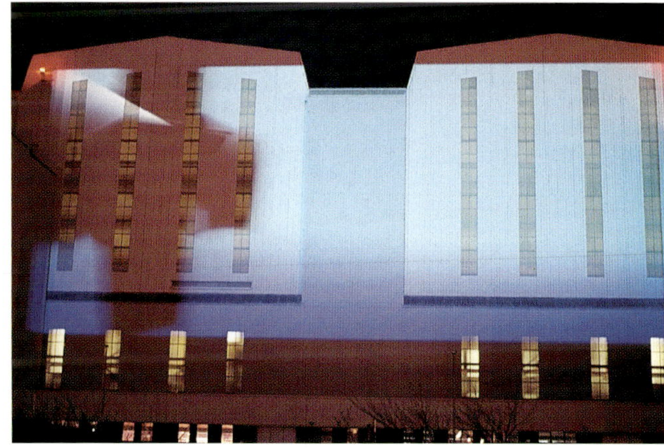

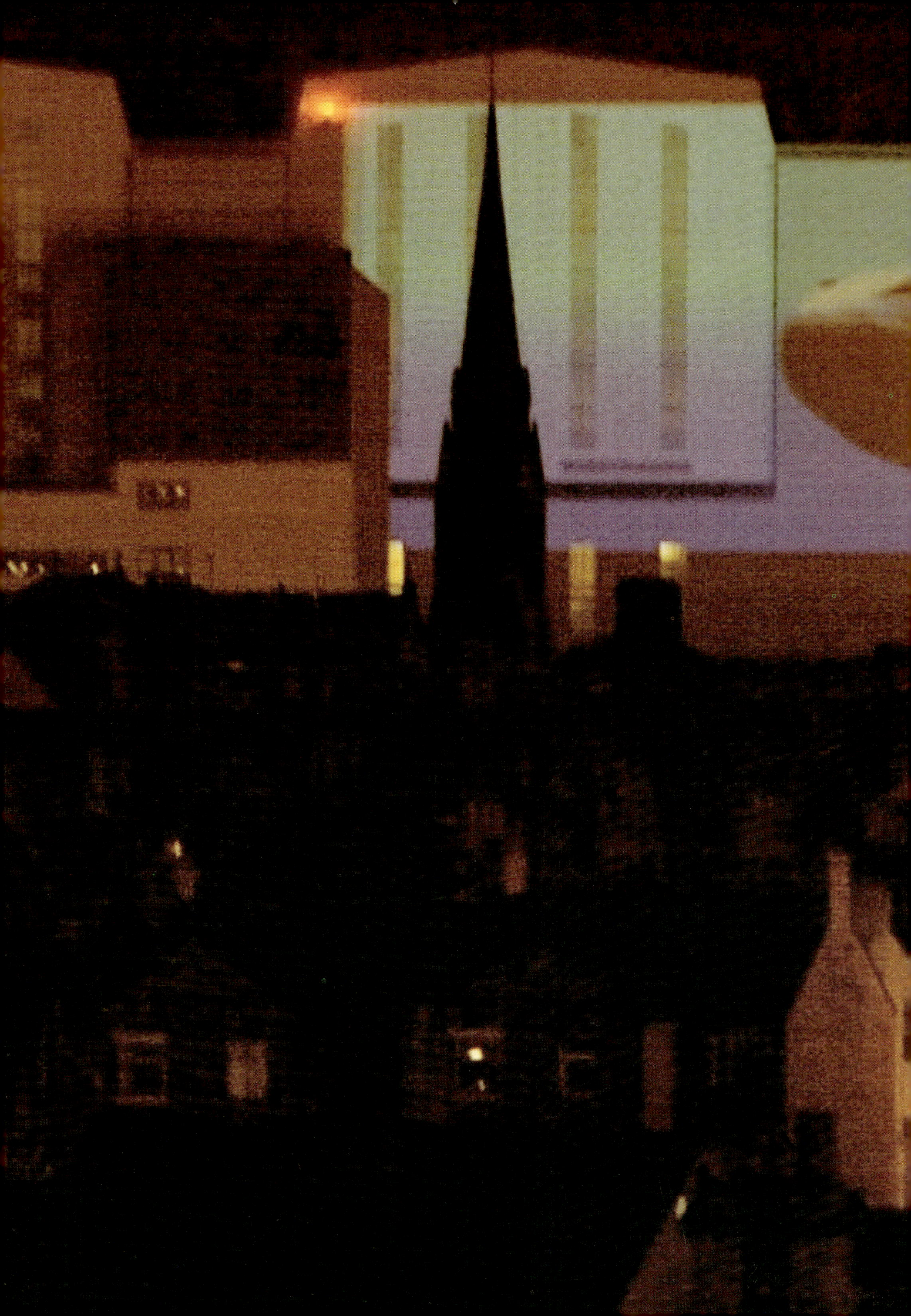

The visual trope of the passing submarine belongs to the world of cinema (*Run Silent Run Deep*, *Das Boot*, etc.). In reality, underwater visibility is so reduced, one would normally be able to see only a detail of the hull at any one time. Gec's projection is a cinematic construction in the mainstream tradition, but re-contextualised to turn back to the origins of its creation. Perhaps it is the link between gigantism, the underwater environment, mystery and visual art that suggests a curious poetic connection between the projection and the following passage from Herman Melville's *Moby Dick*, in which the author describes a painting which, he guesses, may depict a whale impaling itself on the three masts of a ship:

On one side hung a very large oil-painting so thoroughly be-smoked, and every way defaced, that in the unequal cross-lights by which you viewed it, it was only by diligent study and a series of systematic visits to it, and careful enquiry of the neighbours, that you could any way arrive at an understanding of its purpose. Such unaccountable masses of shades and shadows, that at first you almost thought some ambitious young artist, in the time of the New England hags, had endeavoured to delineate chaos bewitched. But by dint of much and earnest contemplation, and oft repeated ponderings, and especially by throwing open the little window towards the back of the entry, you at last come to the conclusion that such an idea, however wild, might not altogether be unwarranted.

But what most puzzled and confounded you was a long, limber, portentous, black mass of something hovering in the centre of the picture over three blue, dim, perpendicular lines floating in a nameless yeast. A boggy, soggy, squitchy picture truly, enough to drive a nervous man distracted. Yet there was a sort of indefinite, half-attained, unimaginable sublimity about it that fairly froze you to it, till you involuntarily took an oath with yourself to find out what that marvellous painting meant. Ever and anon a bright, but, alas, deceptive idea would dart you through. – It's like the Black Sea in a midnight gale. – It's the unnatural combat of the four primal elements. – It's a blasted heath. – It's a Hyberorean winter scene. – It's the breaking-up of the icebound stream of Time... [10]

In classic studies of literature, Captain Ahab has been read as a metaphor for American world domination (the whaling ship driven by an obsessed, cosmic ego – Ahab) and the whale interpreted as the spiritual presence, or God, representing the mysterious Other. As a classic of American nineteenth century epic literature as well as a detailed document of an ancient practice spanning the globe, the themes contained within *Moby Dick* relate well to Gec's interest in global political change, nineteenth and twentieth century tales of empire, the great oceanic system that surrounds us, and the mysterious forces which binds the whole together. [11]

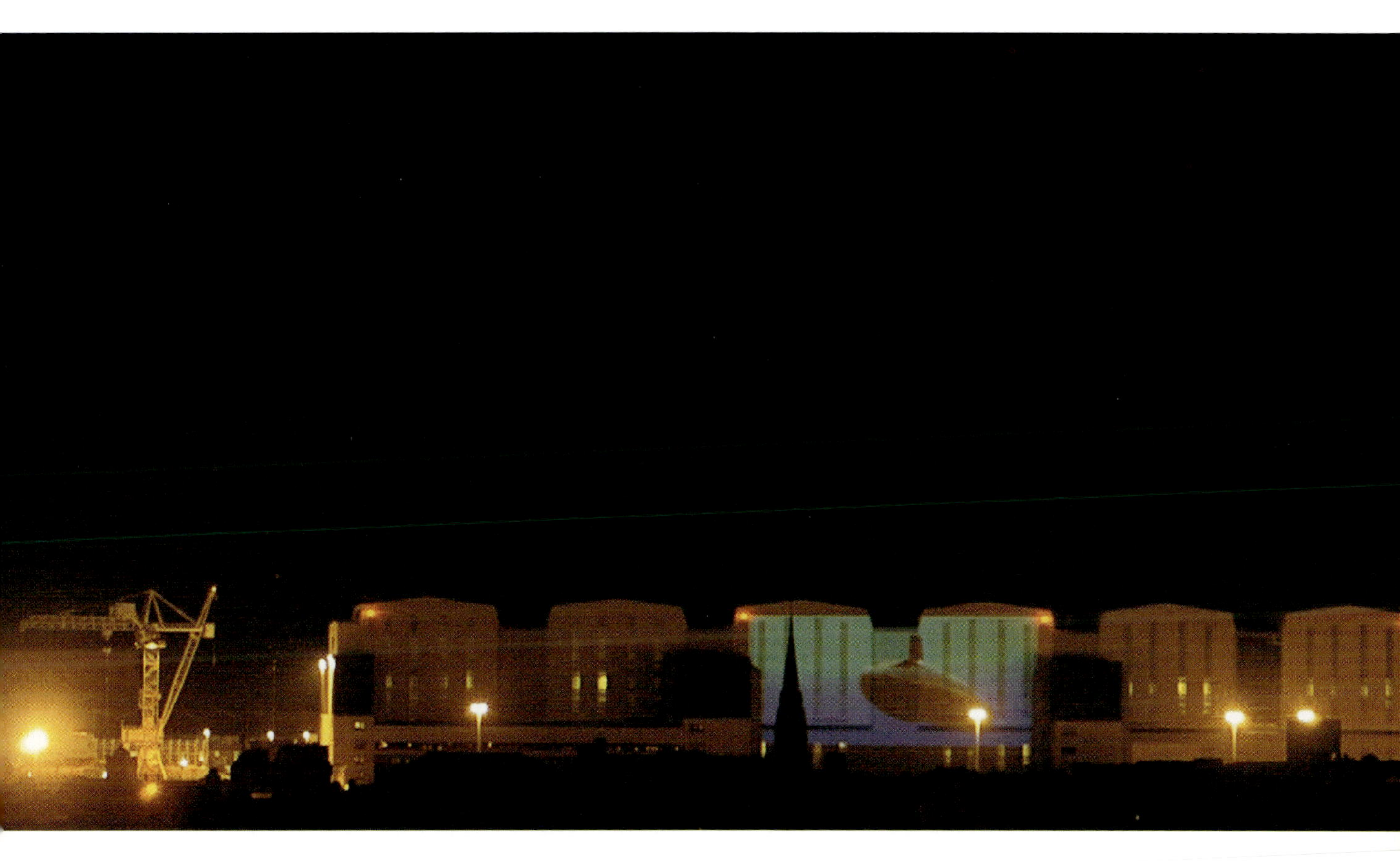

Installation view of the projection,
with Barrow-in-Furness in foreground
Courtesy N.W. Evening Mail

Decompression Chamber

In the context of works concerned with pressure and hostile environments, and among the many works that have been realised by the artist, it is worth accounting for *Decompression Chamber*. It is a fascinating example of a major work in progress – still in a 'world of potentialities'. *Decompression Chamber* remains currently unrealised but first arose as a specific proposal for Chisenhale Gallery, London. The idea centres on placing an operational decompression chamber within a gallery and so creates a decompressed environment within a normal site. *Decompression Chamber* enacts a journey where no physical movement occurs. Those who are used to working professionally with decompression chambers talk of the internal environment of the chamber travelling in time and space, as the pressure slowly rises and falls. In effect another place is created in the gallery – a baromic equivalent to some mysterious depth in the ocean. Despite the work's current life as only a proposal, we can intuit some of its force, partly as an extension of Gec's concern with pressure and demanding environments, but also as a commentary on conventional gallery contexts. Unlike the agendas of oppositional public art, however, Gec plans not merely to reference the external, non-gallery world, or bring his art out of the 'white cube' situation, but instead he aims to create a dramatic, even unwelcoming, place-within-a-place inside the heart of the art world.

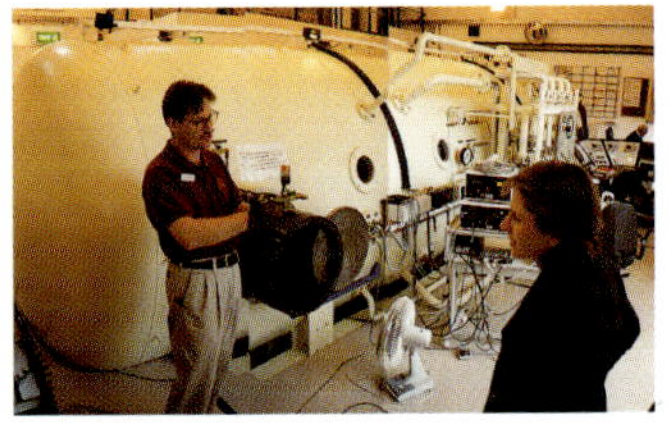

Photographs taken at the Hyperbaric Medical Centre, Plymouth

In terms of methodology, *Decompression Chamber* shows the long developmental process involved in many of Gec's works, starting life as an emergent research project that grows in time, sometimes without a specific commission or site in mind. Technical and informational problems arise that require solutions and these take time. Even realised projects, most clearly represented by the *Trace Elements – Detached Bell Tower – Buoy* sequence of works, change vividly as they move to different stages. The intensive work involved in bringing a project to its moment of first realisation is followed by a pause, perhaps even a genuine end, to that cycle of work. But once the idea has gained a patina as it remains stable for a while, the process often moves on, spurred by a new commission or opportunity. As such, for Gec there is little real distinction between loosely formed ideas, works-in-progress, and completed projects, as each easily offer themselves for development in an iterative way.

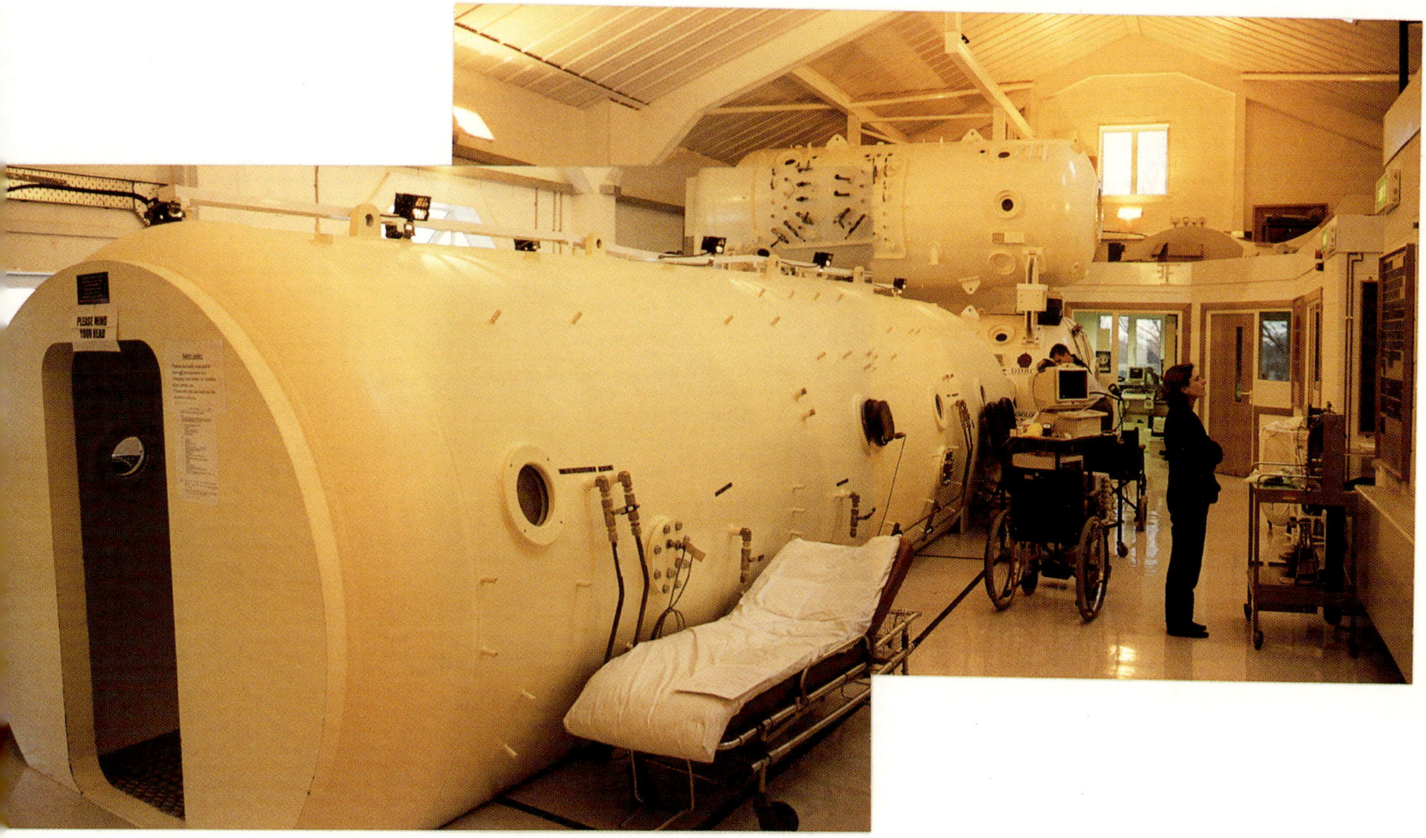

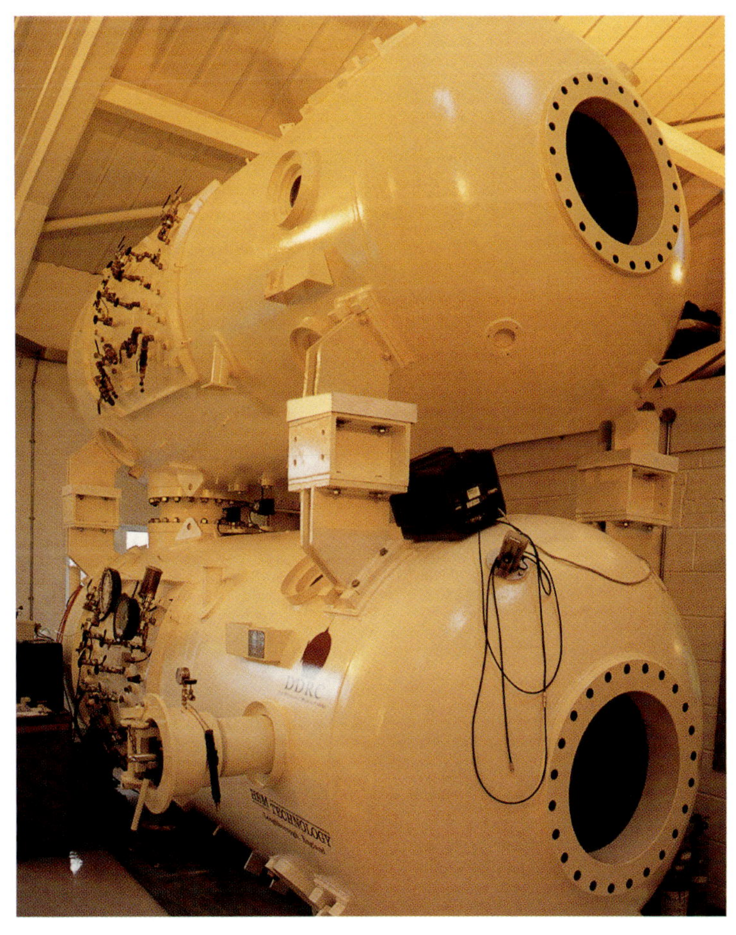
DDRC
HSM TECHNOLOGY

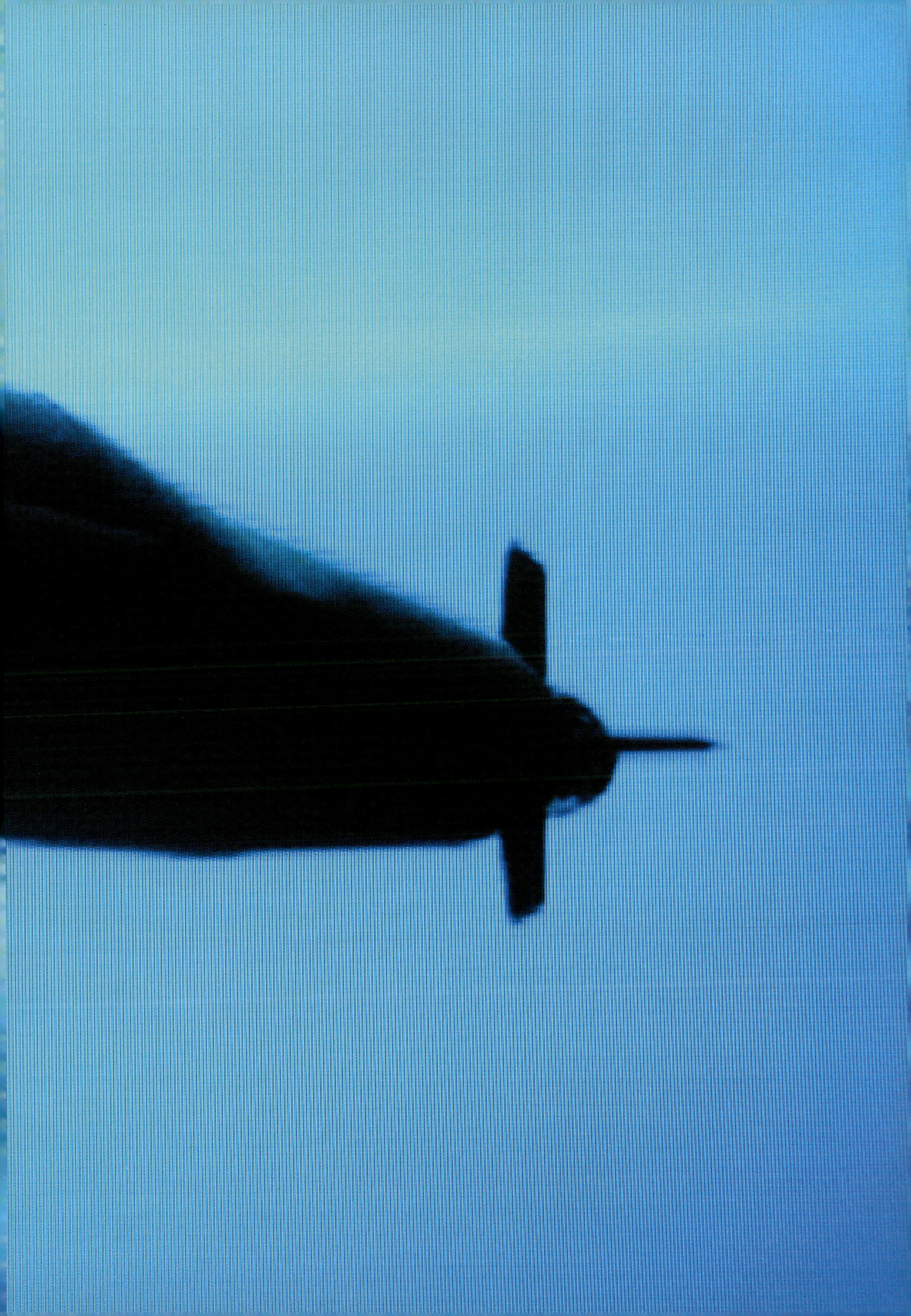

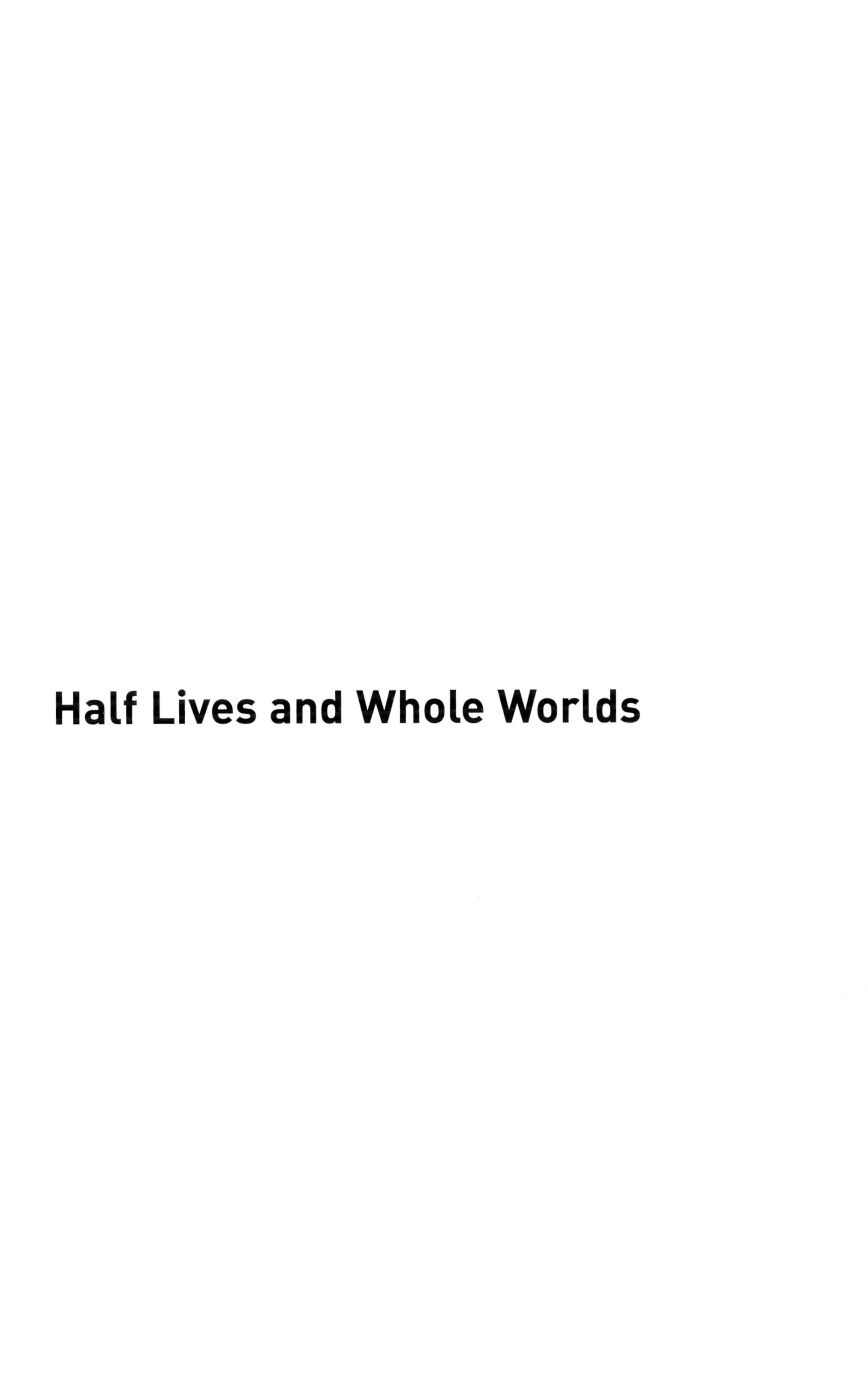

Half Lives and Whole Worlds

Fallout from Chernobyl

The Second World War dispersed populations across Europe and the Americas; Gec's father was a tiny particle of the human fallout. Similarly, many Albanians and Slavs in Britain today arrived in the 1990s following the violent reopening up of ethnic divisions which had festered beneath arbitrary nationalities imposed on them throughout this century. In this context we can appreciate the emotional as well as poetic impact on Gec when, at 1.24 am on Saturday 26 April 1986, the Chernobyl nuclear plant in the Ukraine exploded following an error in the shutdown procedure in Block 4.

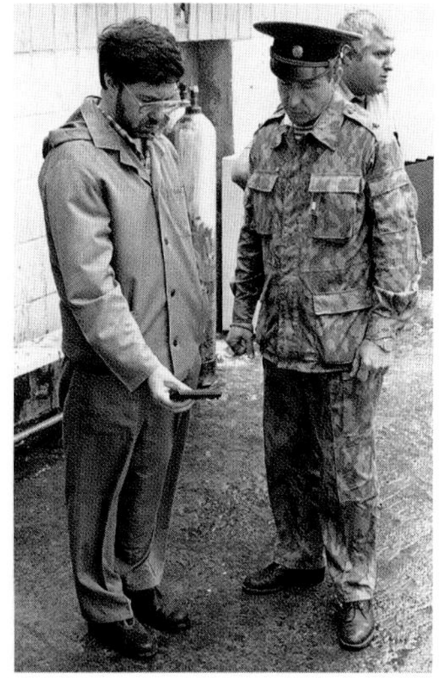

Taking a Geiger Counter reading outside Chernobyl's Fire Station

Above Opposite: Cots inside an abandoned nursery, Pripyat

Below Opposite: Fire engine and memorial, Chernobyl
(the mark, top left, was made by a radioactive particle coming into contact with the negative)

Following pages: Derelict nursery, Pripyat

It is clear from the brief diaries Gec wrote when he visited the site in 1995, that he sensed Chernobyl and nearby Pripyat were still locked in time by the events of 1986:

The van passed through the city centre of Pripyat. Rows upon rows of high rise flats, shops, a large hotel, a ferris wheel in the distance. We climbed out of the van into the silent city. Thousands of empty windows looked down at us. Telephone boxes sat on the street corners. We gathered under a sign over a government building doorway which read INTO LIFE. In 1986 President Gorbachev used this as part of his perestroika speeches in the historic resolutions of the XXVII Party Congress. Chernobyl is trapped in time. A truck rumbled in the distance. [12]

Gec is clearly responding here to the 30 km exclusion zone around Chernobyl, the equivalent of an 'airlock' beyond which no one could go. The themes of dislocation, entrapment, and the transformation of geographical space were key to the artist. He is often interested in subjects where it is possible for physical space to be torn from its moorings and deposited elsewhere. What one might term the 'psycho-geographics' of Chernobyl was to spur Gec on to many major works.

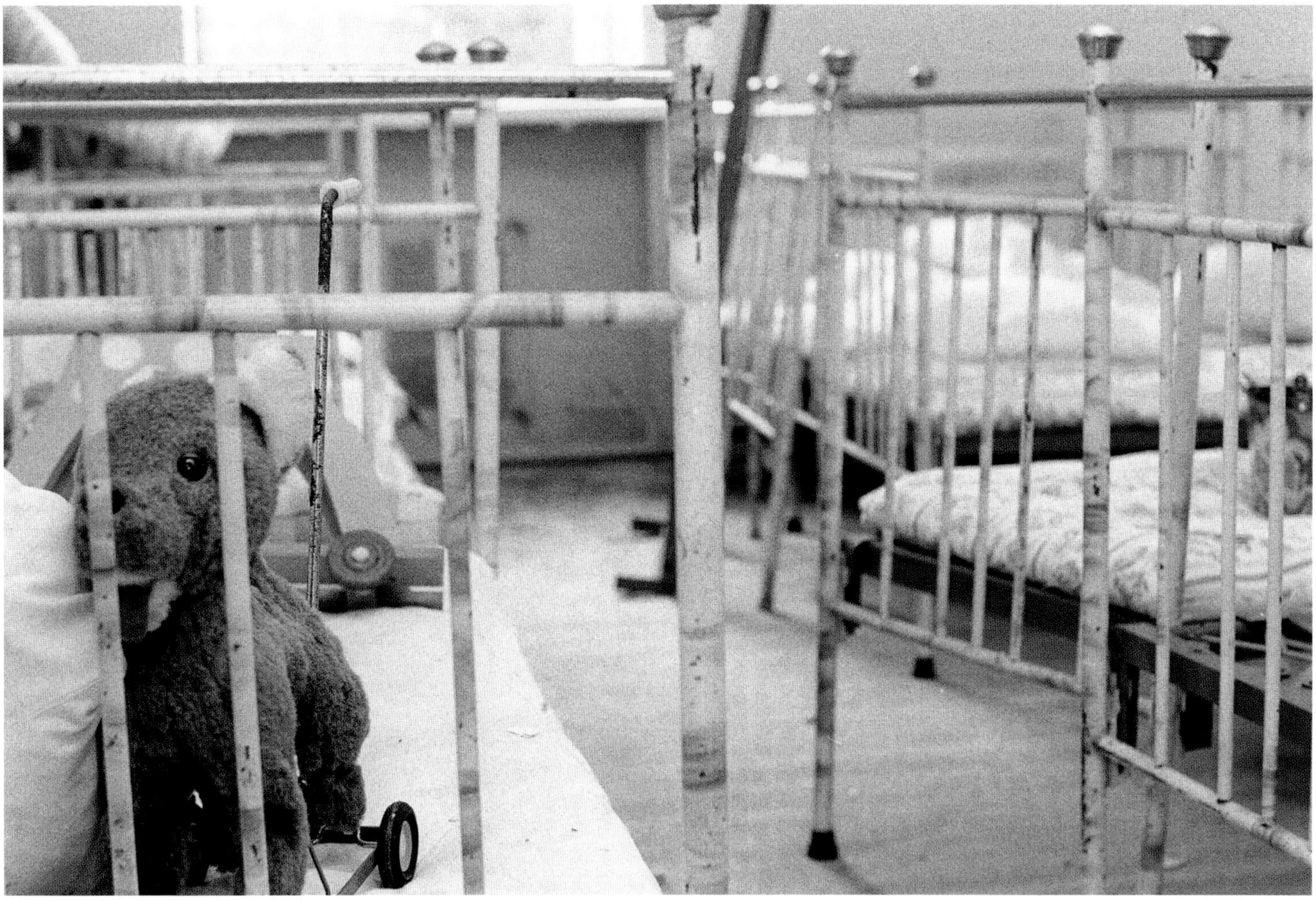

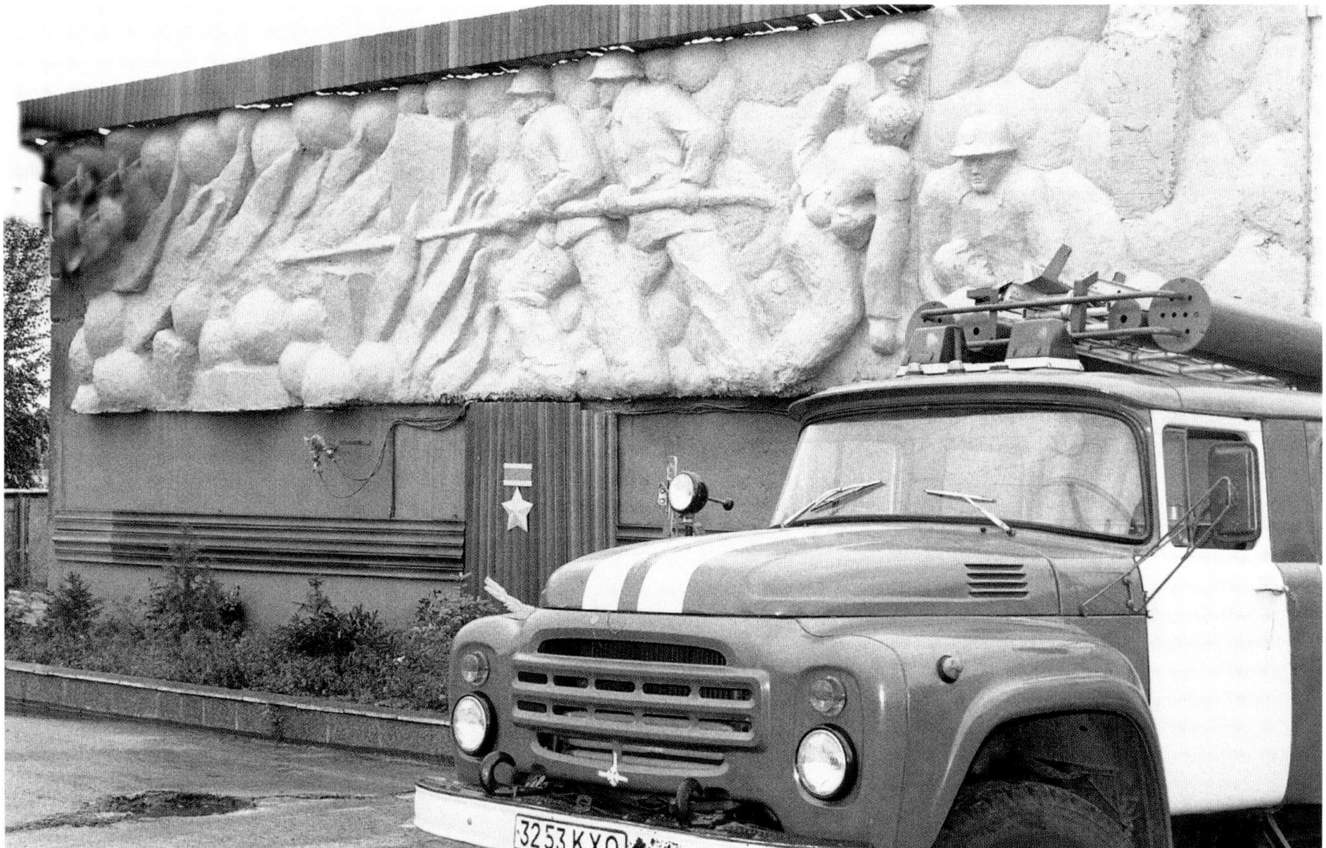

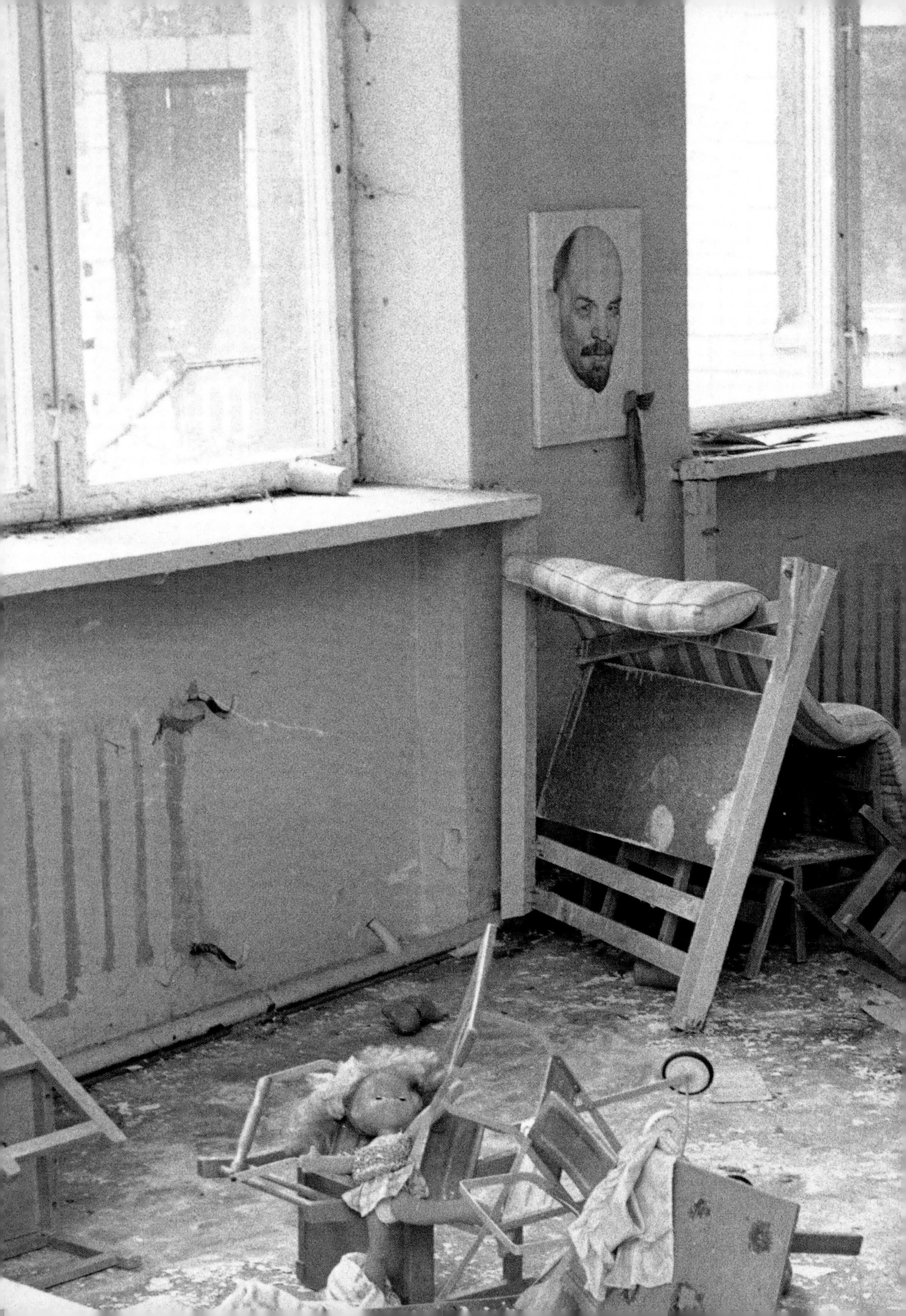

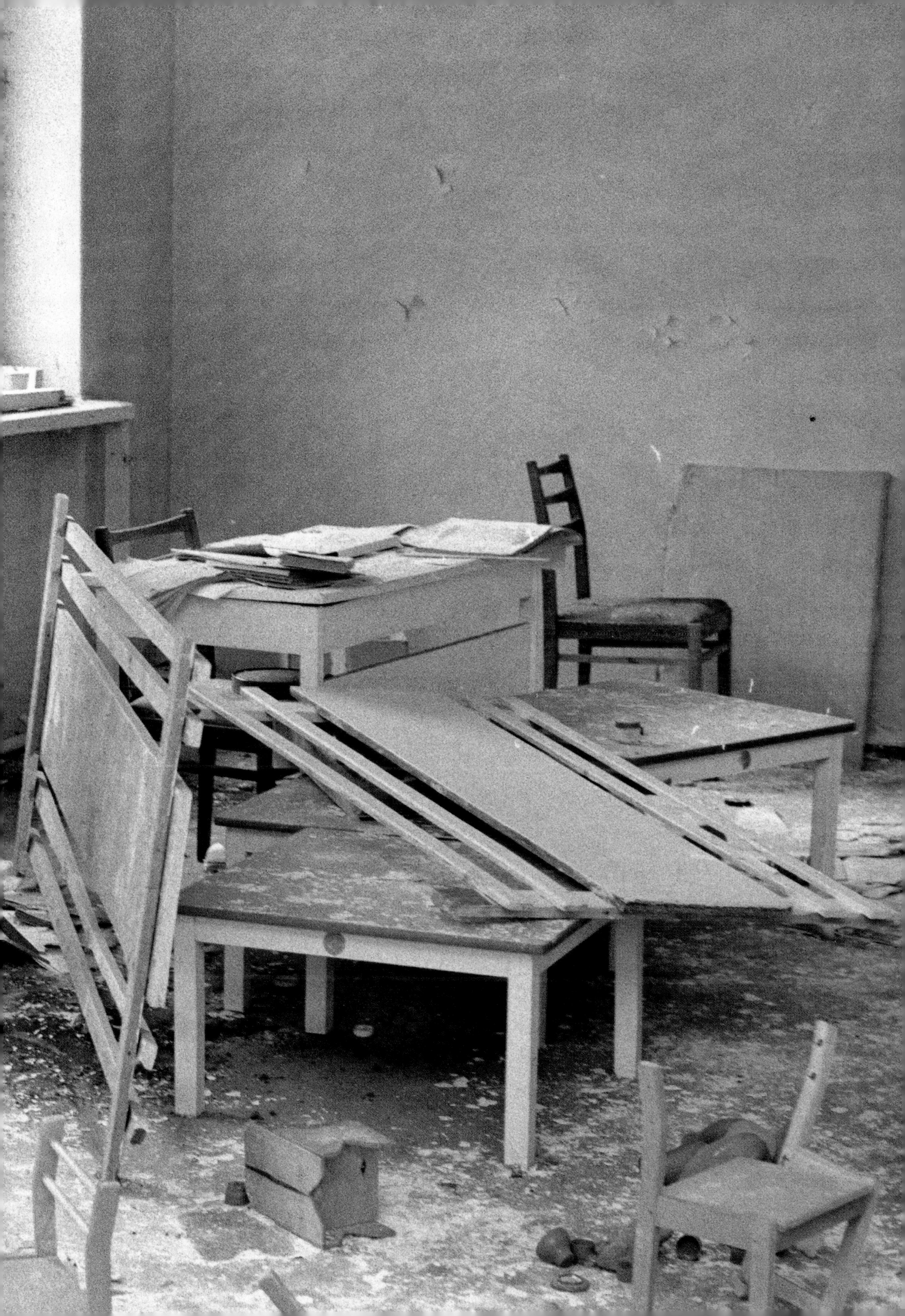

Cattle grazing at Chernobyl's research centre

Following pages: Pripyat's deserted city centre

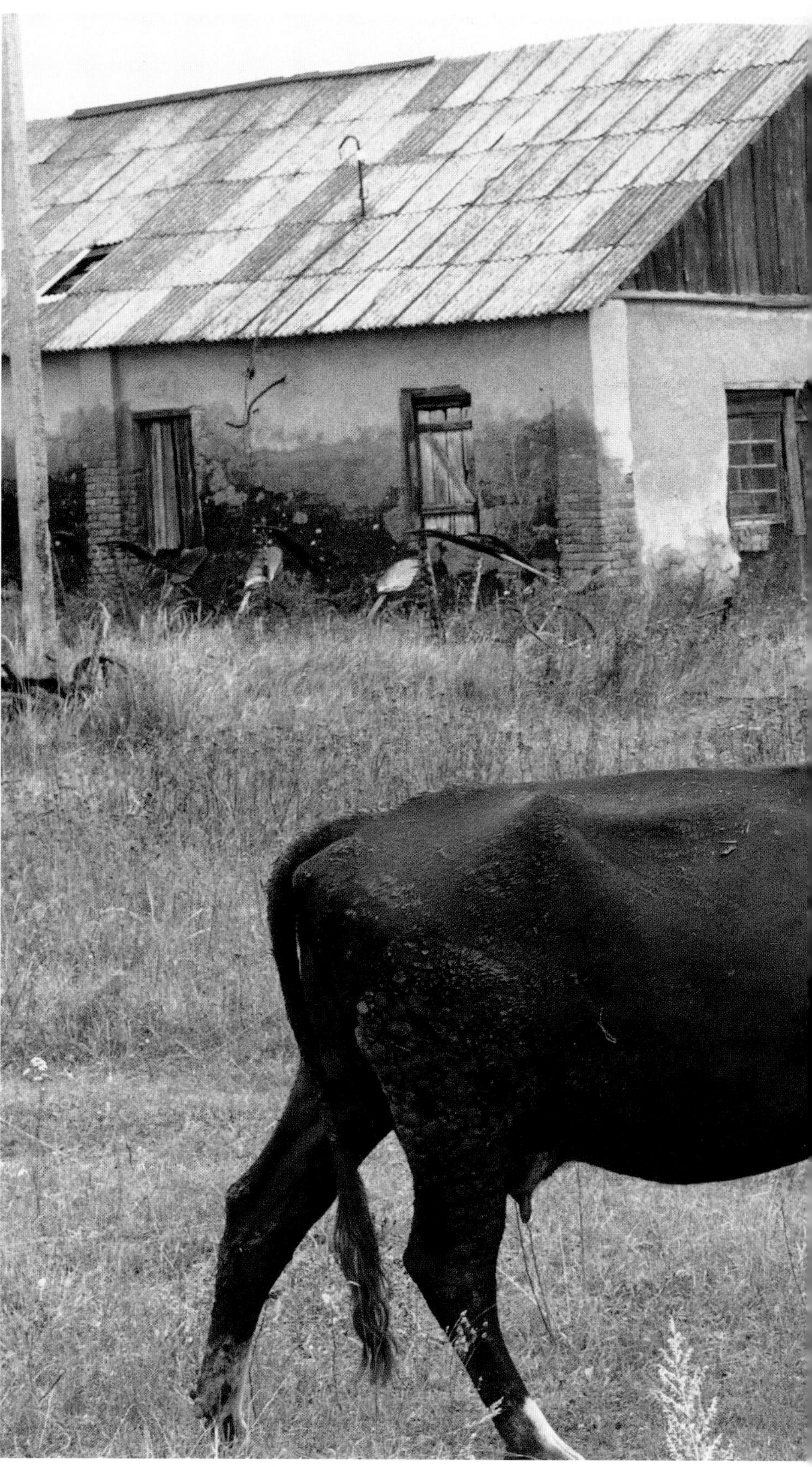

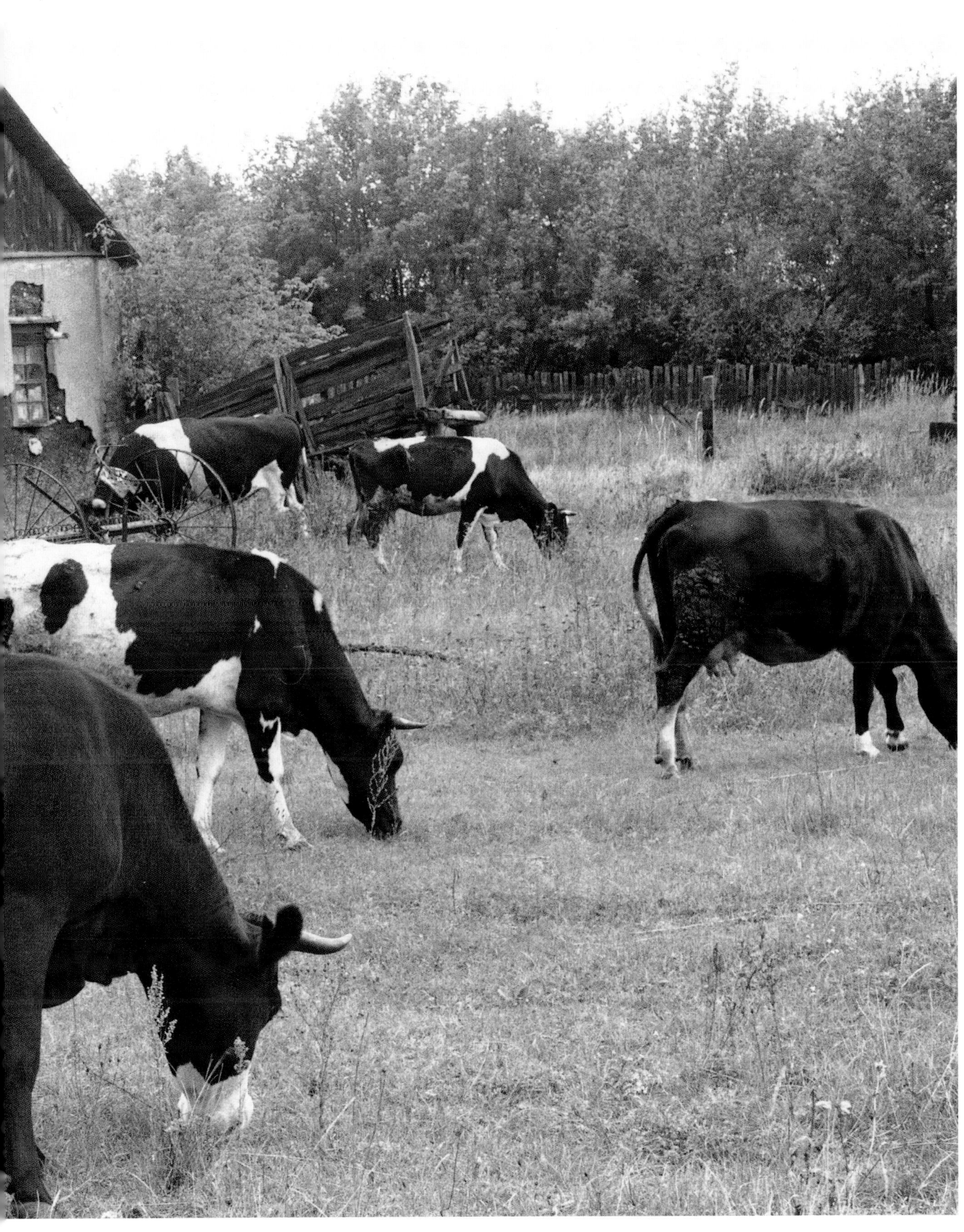

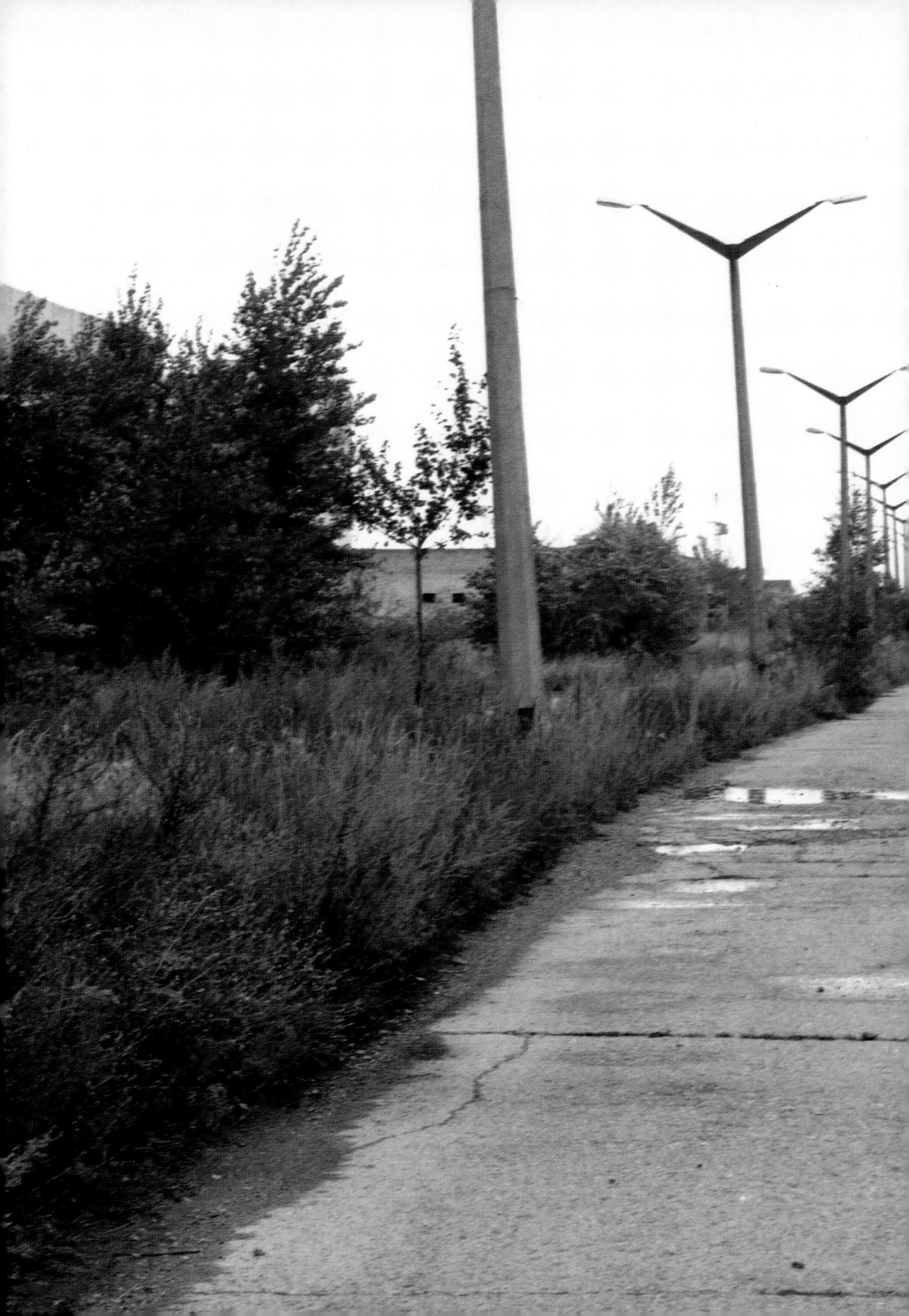

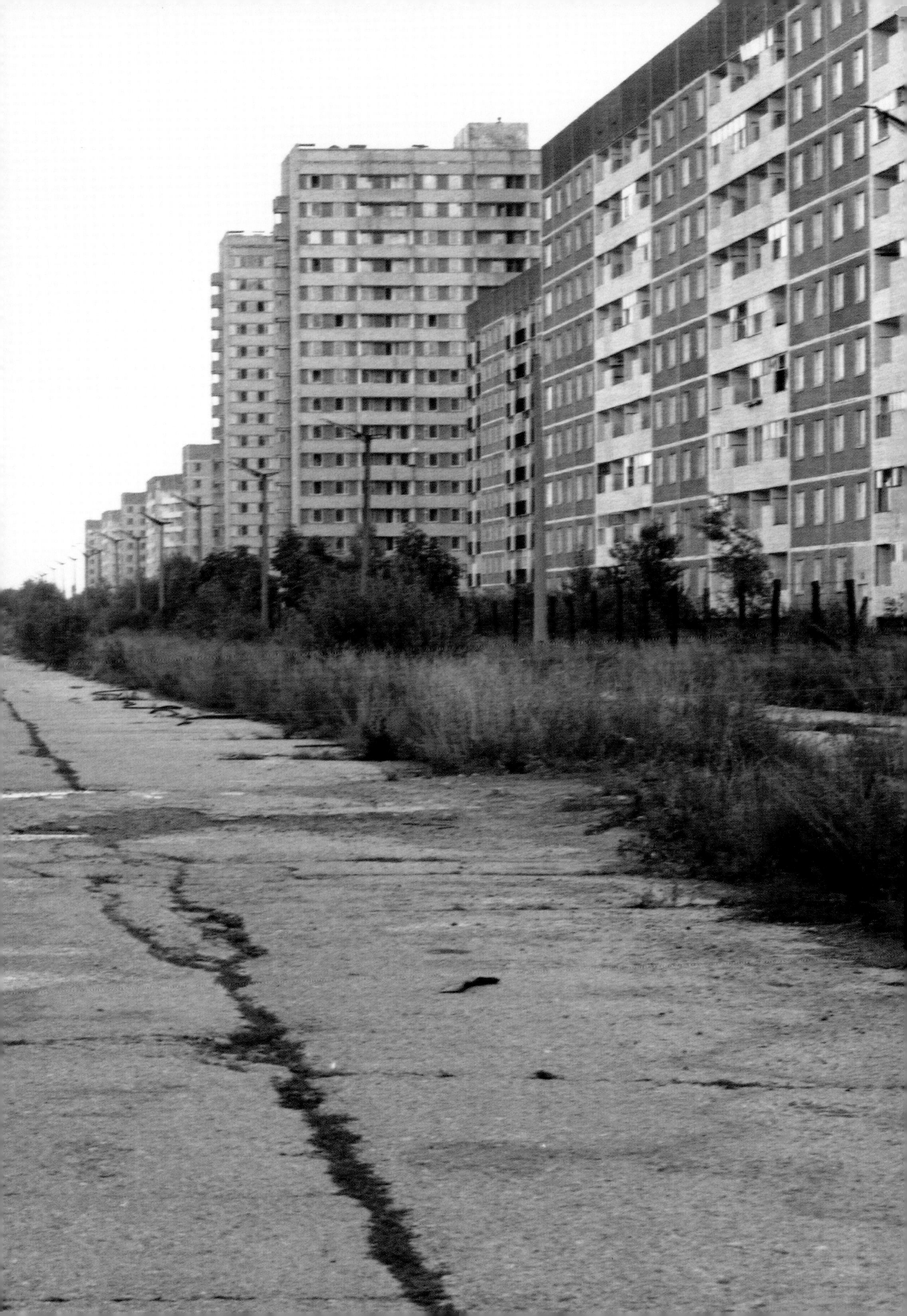

Bitter Waters

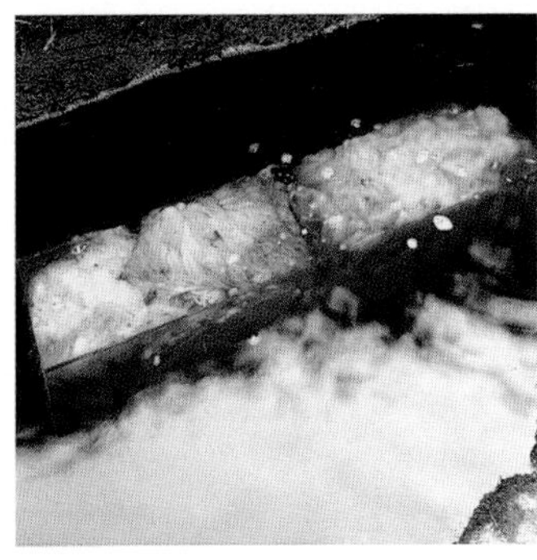

Washing the fleeces in one of the feeder streams at Cow Green

Opposite: *Bitter Waters*, 1990, wool and Ukrainian embroidery

Following pages: Placing the container in the feeder streams and water draining after washing the fleeces at Cow Green

Gec's first work in relation to Chernobyl was a performance called *Bitter Waters*, undertaken in the North of England on the fourth anniversary of the accident in 1990. He separately washed a fleece from Cumbria and one from Northumbria in Cow Green reservoir through which ran the border between the two counties and acknowledged officially to be contaminated by Chernobyl nuclear fallout. The fleece was woven into two woollen panels, joined in the centre by a length of Ukrainian embroidery. The work alludes to the elusive boundary between what might be considered the 'centre' and the 'periphery'. Clouds into which the immediate radioactive material was thrown carried the most toxic elements away from the disaster zone and broadcast it first into Scandinavia, followed by Britain, Central Europe and the Balkans (though changing weather conditions meant that virtually all of Europe was affected). *Bitter Waters*, as with the following commission *Natural History*, demonstrates on many levels how climate and catastrophe combine in ways that are ignorant of national boundaries. Gec's somewhat haphazard family history which created a route from the Ukraine to the North East of England was retraced decades later by the poisonous caesium-137 which, equally haphazardly, followed in the rain clouds. Indeed it was rainfall which brought the radioactive material to earth and through its eventual absorption into vegetation and subsequent consumption by sheep, proved to be the most devastating vehicle of transmitting contamination into the human food chain; hence Gec's combined use of sheep fleece and water. At the time the Western media attempted to 'contain' this disaster themselves, through the perception that we were merely witnessing the old Soviet Bloc nuclear industry cracking, deep across its rust belt. The implication from the West was that such neglect and carelessness could simply never happen here. Inevitably, the Chernobyl disaster saw both political and national agendas being played out, but it also witnessed more subtle ones, which speak of the porous and temporary boundaries that inscribe our lives wherever we live on this planet.

Through *Bitter Waters*, Gec was also able to explore the wider implications of 'contamination', or the invisible spread of one dangerous or threatening element to other places. Through the creation of a relatively simple artefact, he made visible the way in which two places are brought together – in this case Ukraine and Northern England. Subsequently, contamination has become for Gec a powerful metaphor for the irrelevance of borders.

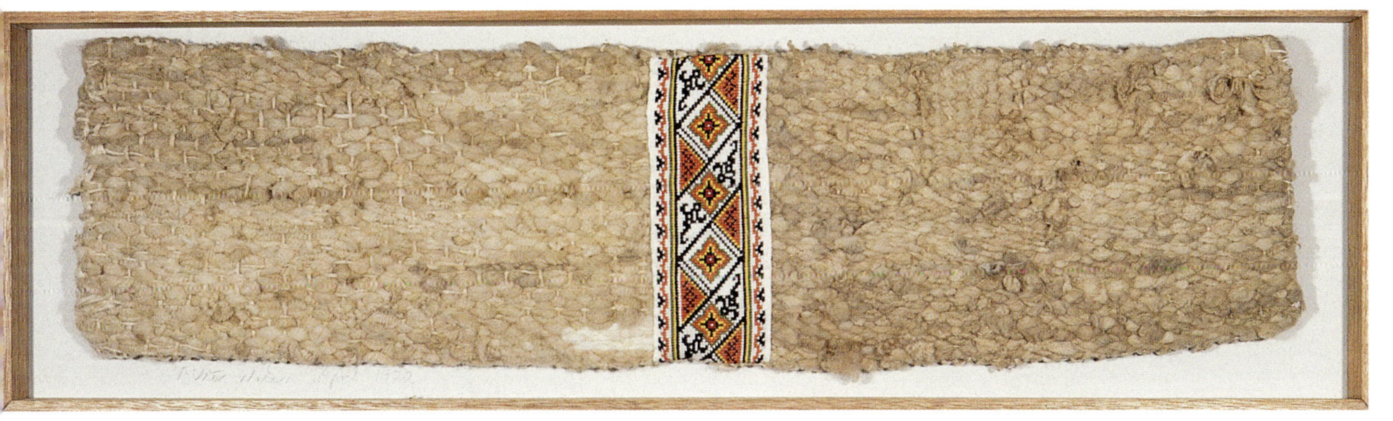

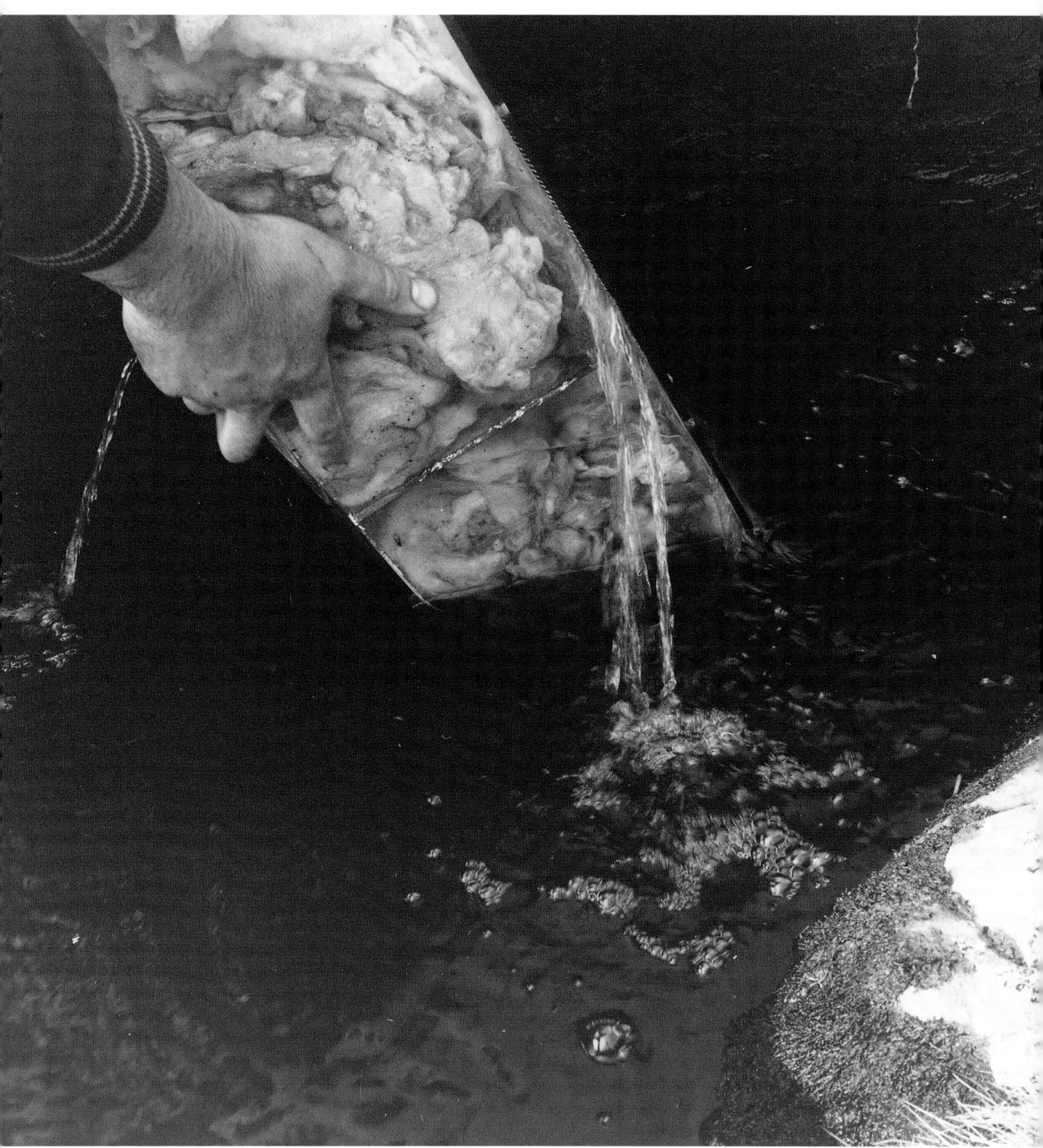

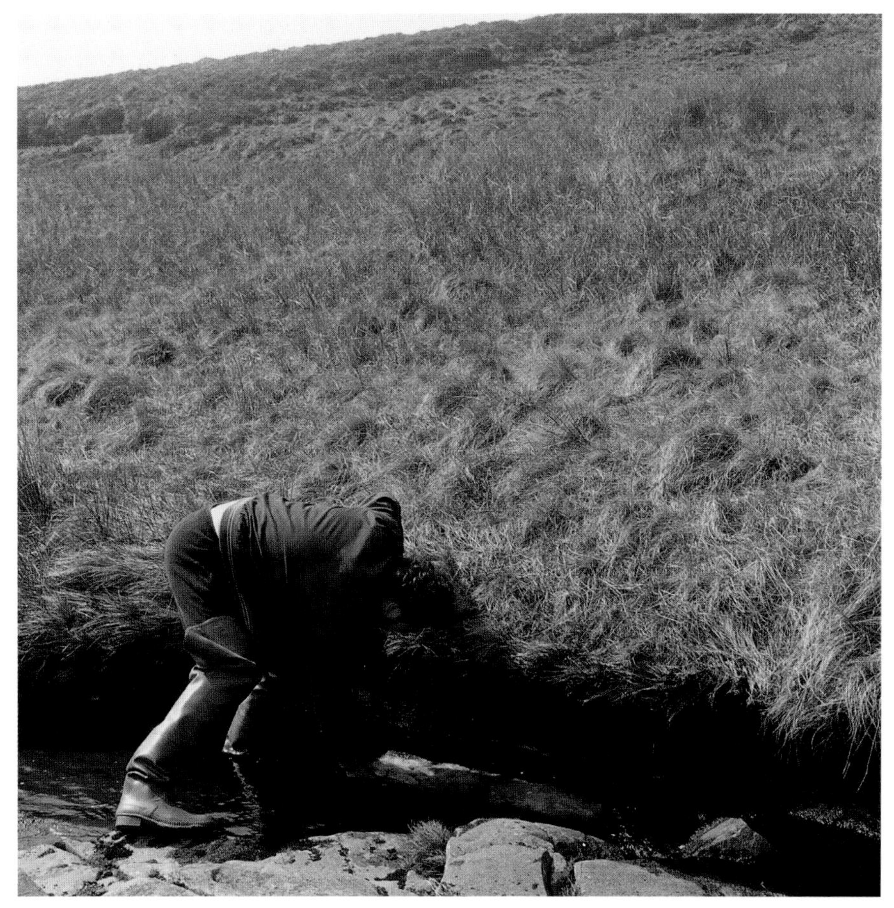

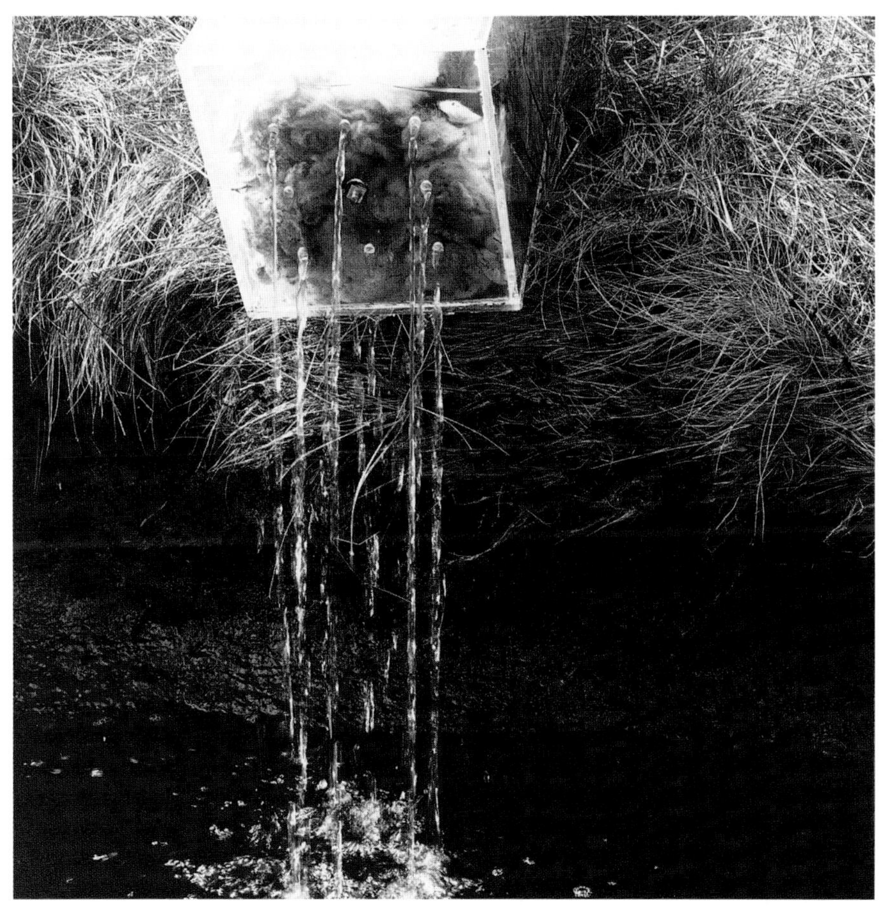

Natural History

Contamination, family ties, industrialisation out of control, and heroism: these are just some the issues that lie below the surface of the major single project inspired by Chernobyl, *Natural History*, 1995. It was installed on the roof of Pilgrim Street Fire Station, Newcastle upon Tyne on the ninth anniversary of the disaster, and just four months before Gec made his first visit to his father's homeland. Whilst watching the TV news Gec became aware that a delegation from the Chernobyl and Pripyat fire-brigades, who heroically stopped the fires overnight but suffered most from radiation poisoning as a consequence, were repaying a visit by firemen from Newcastle made to the Ukraine immediately after the disaster. Researching the event, Gec came across small portrait photographs of the first six firemen killed in the immediate aftermath of the fire. These images, of course, soon became buried in the popular conscience as the impact of Chernobyl dissipated like the radioactive particles themselves. By reprinting them and publicly displaying them on top of the fire station as 4.5 x 3 metre scanachrome photographs, Gec sought to reinstate the prominence of those six firemen: Nikolai Vasilievich Vashchuk, Vasilii Ivanovich Ignatenko, Victor Nikolaevich Kibenok, Vladimir Pavlovich Pravik, Nikolai Ivanovich Titenok and Vladimir Ivanovich Tishchura. It is not by accident that the proportions he chose for this work were similar to banners on which the faces of political leaders in Soviet countries were paraded through the streets.

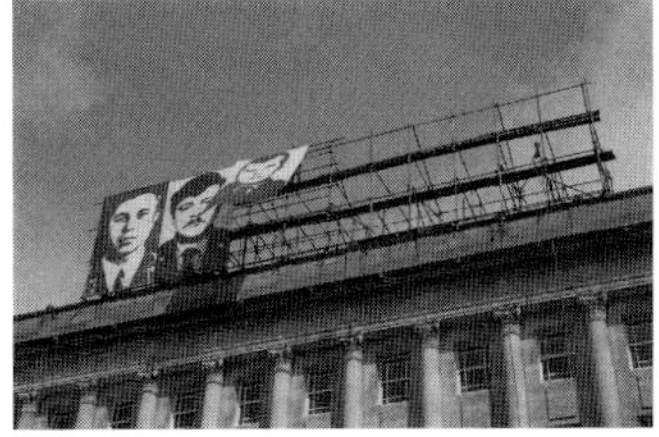

Installing *Natural History*

Opposite: *Natural History*, 1995
Pilgrim Street Fire Station
Newcastle upon Tyne

Following pages: Photographs found in an abandoned house within the 30 km exclusion zone around Chernobyl

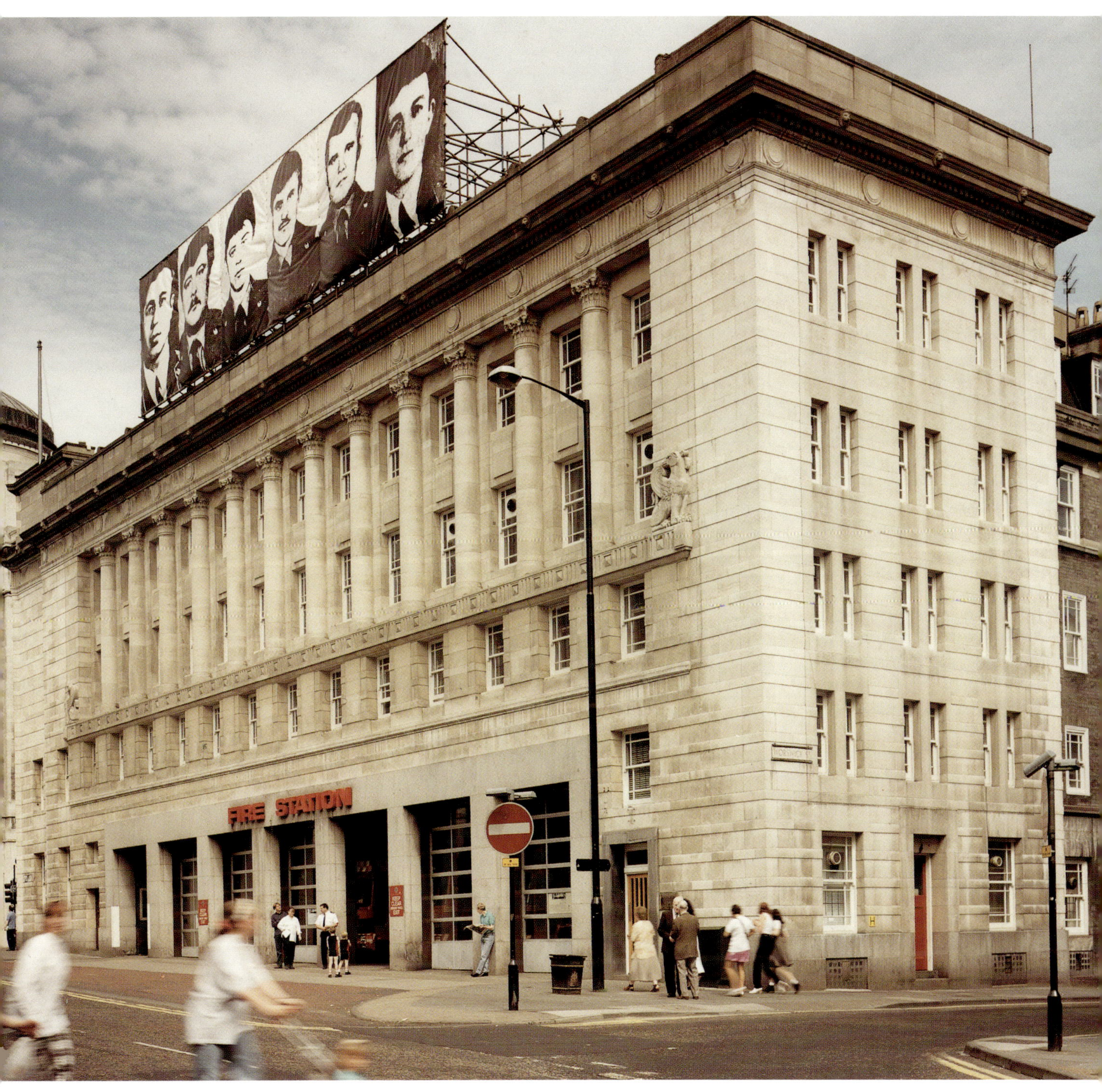

Natural History 1995

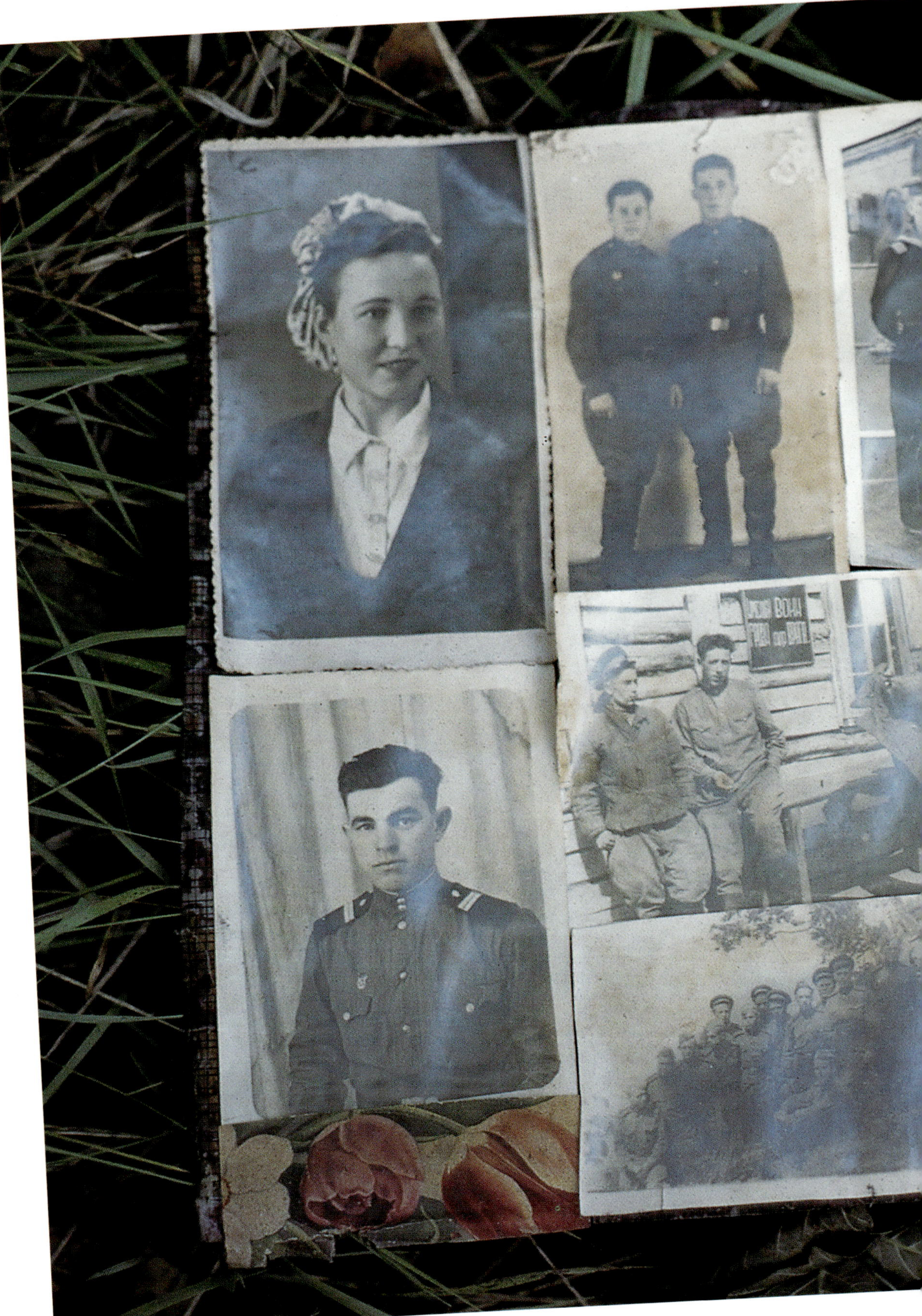

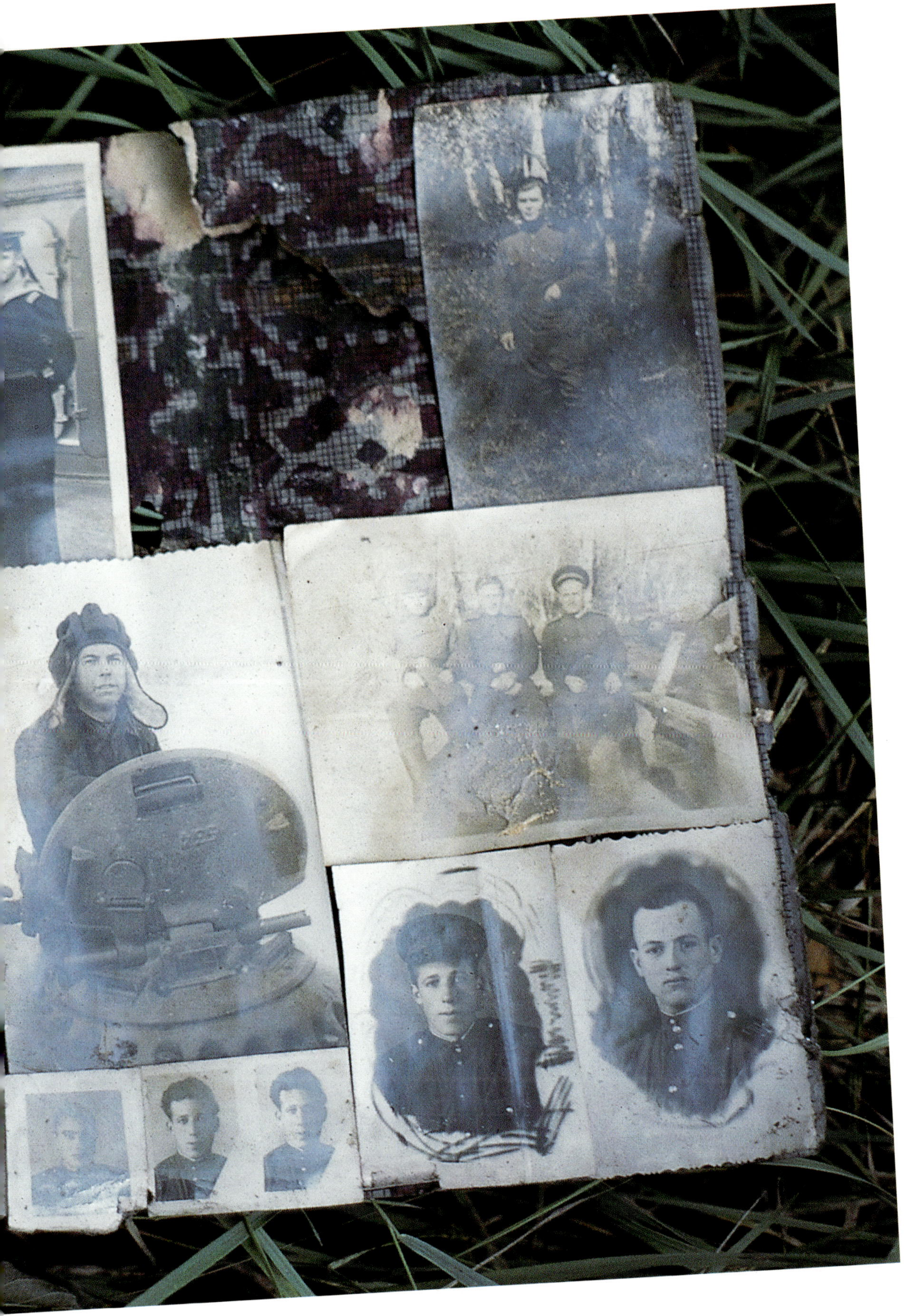

Given that Gec's art is concerned with conditions of movement and change as they manifest themselves, he clearly understands that by installing projects in other countries their meaning unavoidably alters. Perhaps not surprisingly, the siting of *Natural History* outside the Ukrainian Cultural and Education Centre in Winnipeg, Canada was received uncomfortably by some among the large ex-patriot population who live there today, due mainly to its mimicking conventional depiction's of Soviet heroes and religious icons. In the 1960s the Artists' Placement Group in Britain adopted the useful, if somewhat arbitrary, equation that "the context is half the work" in the laudable aim to erase the formal singularity of modern art, and certainly we might see Gec's work as illustrative of how contextual changes amend or reposition meaning. Whilst all artists have no more than partial control over many of the contextual factors bearing down on their work, Gec is at least one artist who makes work in the explicit knowledge that meaning relates both to the geographic and psychological positioning of art.

Natural History, 1995, (detail)
fireman Vasilii Ivanovich Ignatenko

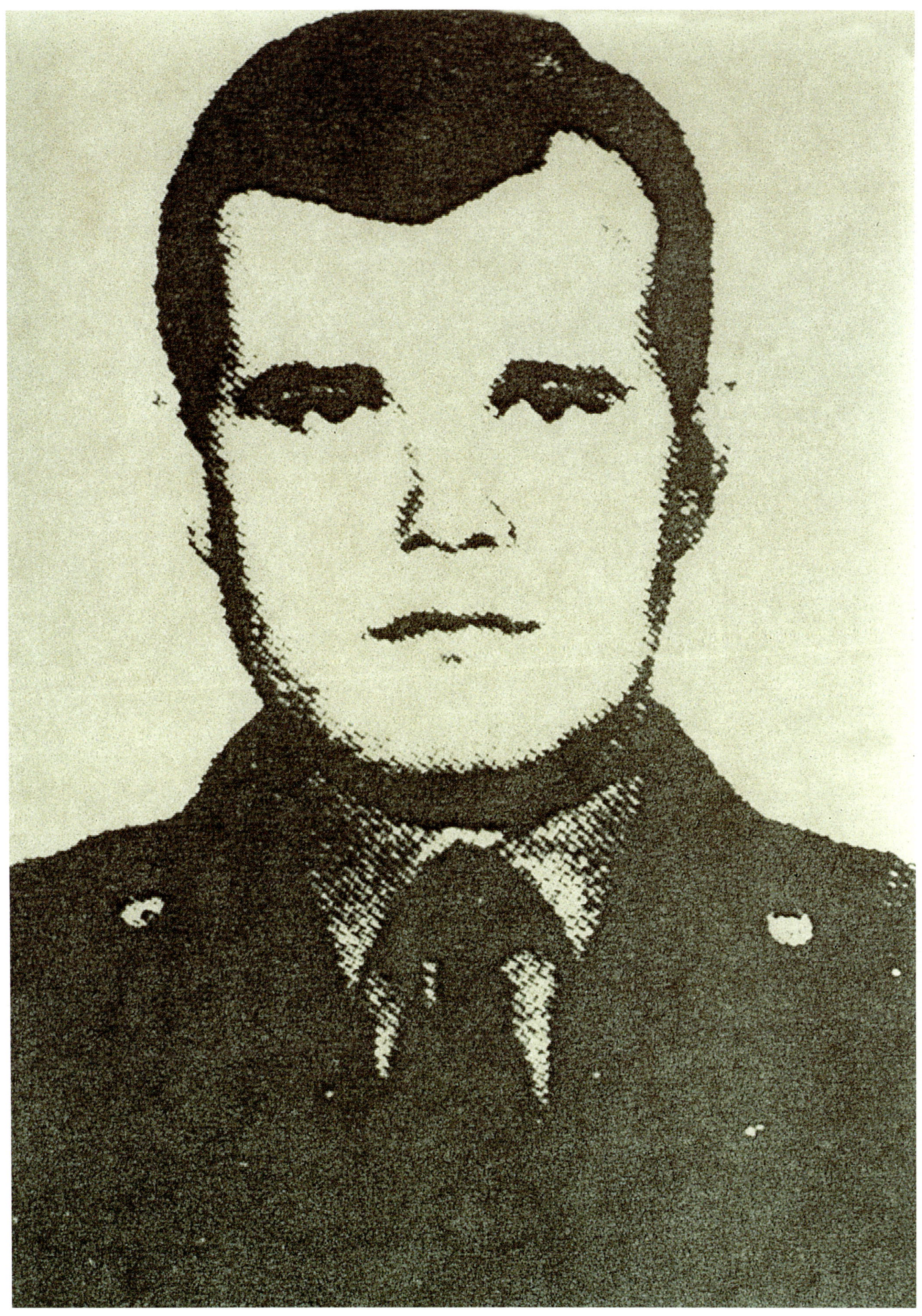

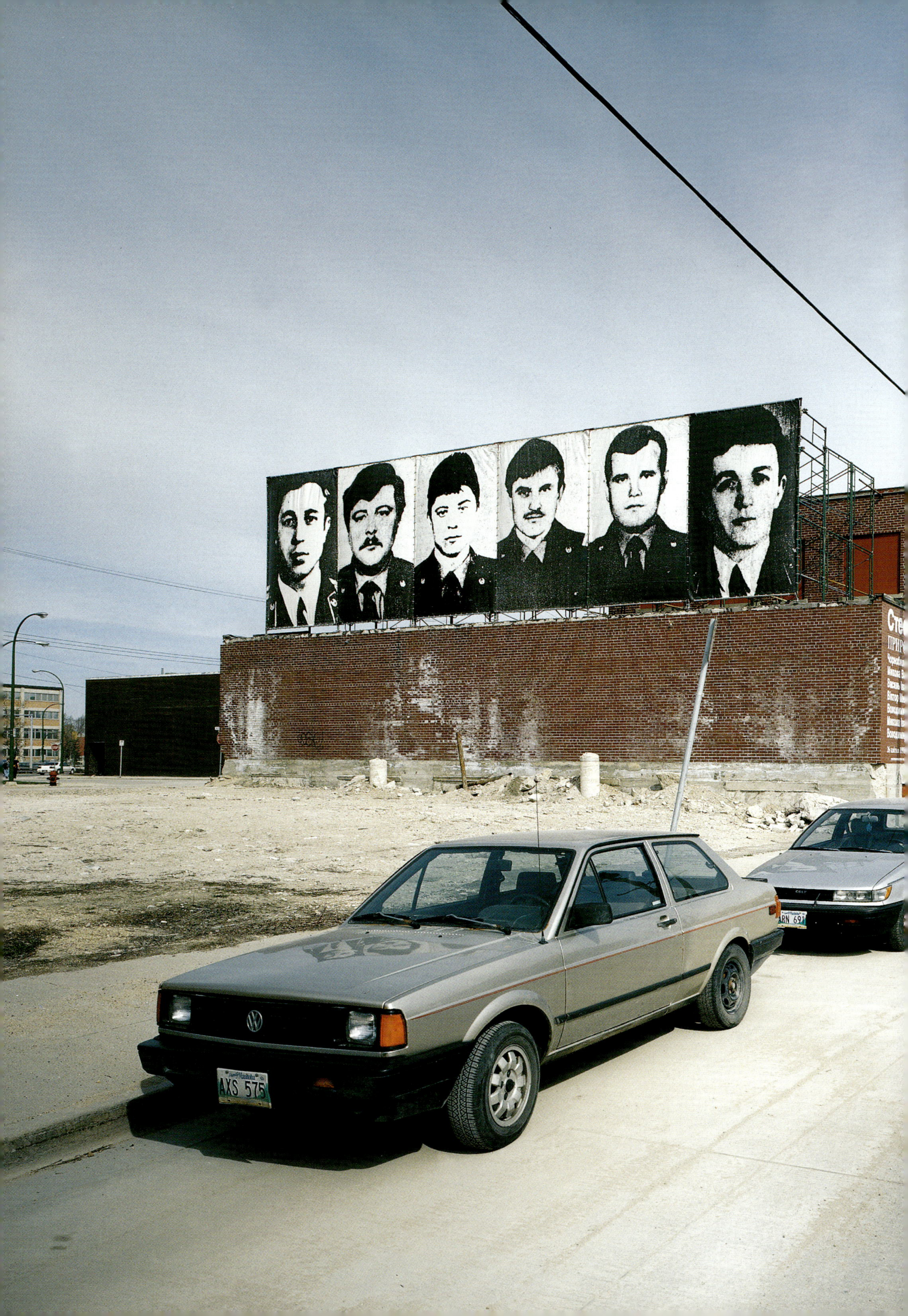

AXS 575

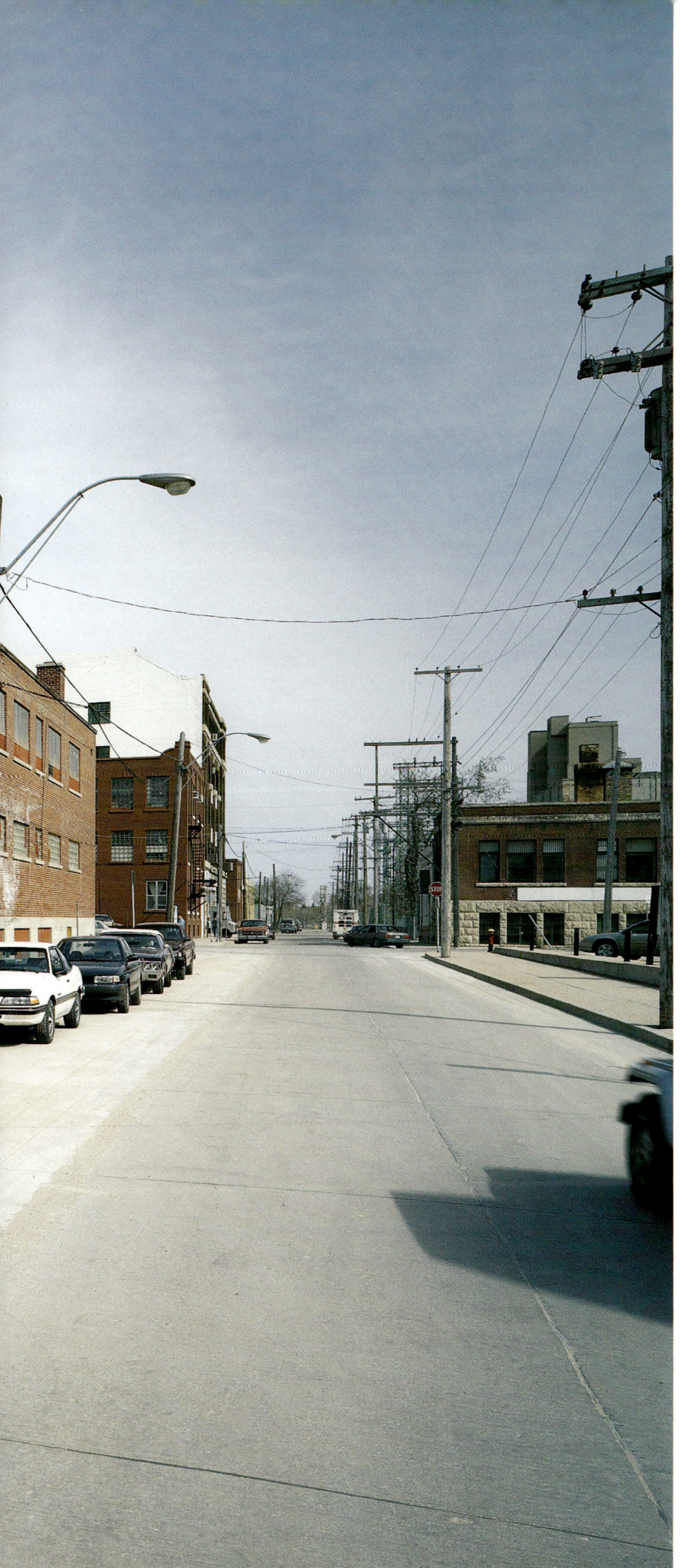

Natural History,
Ukrainian Cultural Centre,
Winnipeg, 1998

Trace Elements

Before we come to Gec's increasingly ambitious and continuing project, *Buoy*, we must consider two related works which preceded it, namely *Trace Elements* and *Detached Bell Tower*. *Trace Elements* began with the discovery in 1990 that eight Soviet Whisky Class submarines were being scrapped at a former decommissioning yard, Battleship Wharf in Blyth, north of Newcastle upon Tyne. Documentary photographs of the submarines in Blyth show them abandoned, tied up and desultory, visually not unlike a haul of dead whales. The identification of this moment in time is a good example of the artist's receptive instinct, in finding a situation – marking a moment – within which he can act; especially as we now know that 1989/90 saw the first edifices of the Soviet Union and Eastern Bloc being physically dismantled. The scrapped submarines at Blyth were a small by-product of the massive political upheaval taking place in the East. The artist intercepted and arranged for eight steel sections of each submarine hull to be cut away and from which eight large bells were cast. The inert salvaged steel was to find life again in a completely different form. The resulting bells were installed on a wooden pontoon surrounding one leg of the High Level Bridge above the River Tyne in the centre of Newcastle upon Tyne. They were suspended at a level from purpose-built wooden spars, which at low tide held them up fully visible above the water. At high tide the water submerged them into invisibility. With great formal simplicity, Gec achieved a remarkable transformation. With the military potency of the submarines now lost, their metal daily rose and fell above the water line, just as they did as working boats. The form and function of the bells situated under the bridge was a striking part of the work. They were either suspended in space, heavy and silent unable to sound out, or submerged beneath the waves where the clappers, moved by the flow of the tide, were only able to send muffled vibrations out into the Tyne and beyond. Similarly, in choosing to cast the hull metal into bells, the artist deliberately points to ritual and religion as well as setting up more poetic associations concerning long-distance communication.

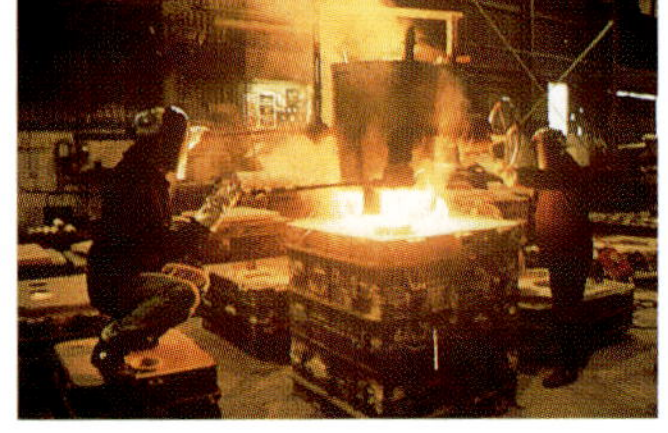

Trace Elements, steel being poured into a mould

Opposite: Whisky Class submarines moored at Battleship Wharf, Blyth

Following pages: Breaking the submarines for scrap

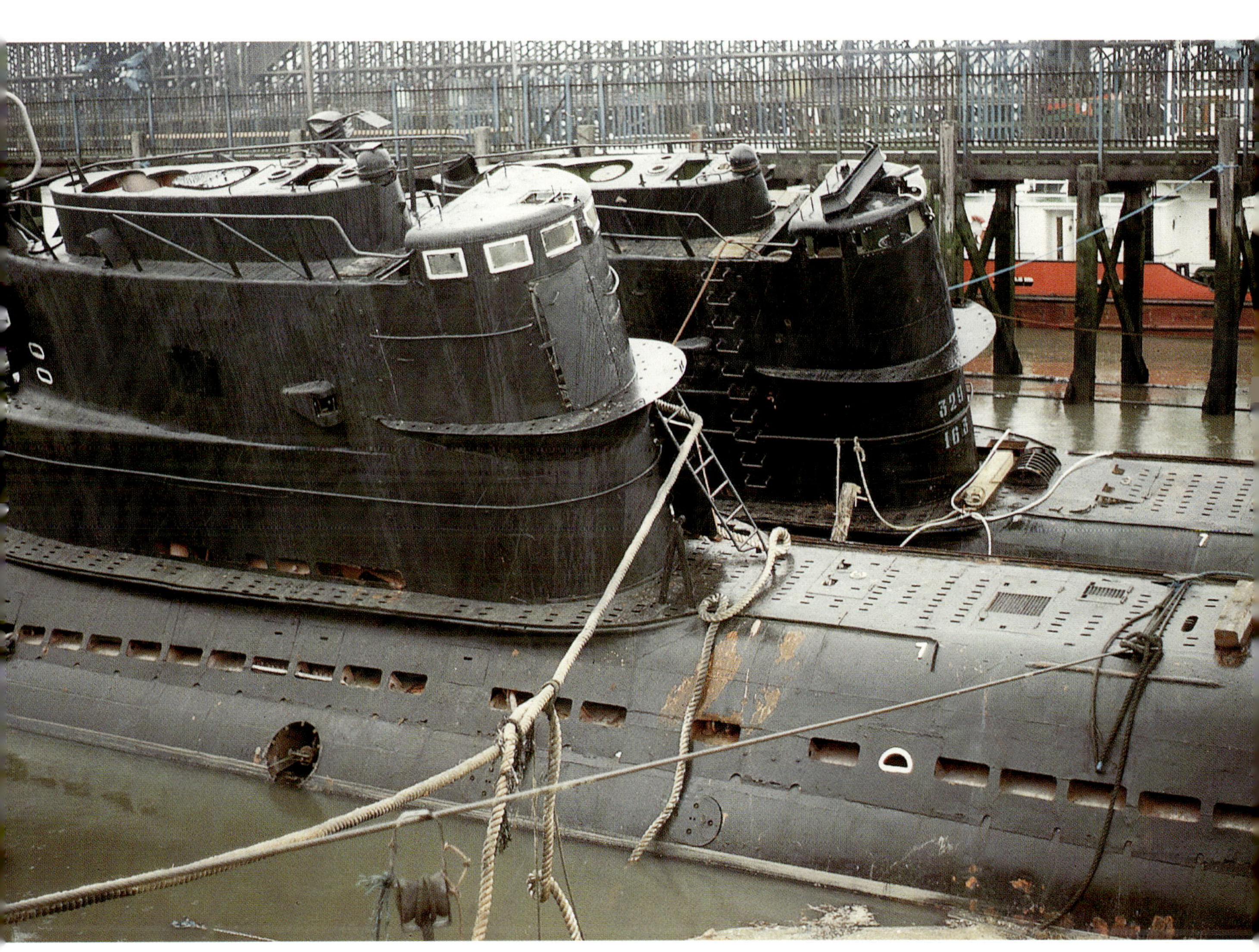

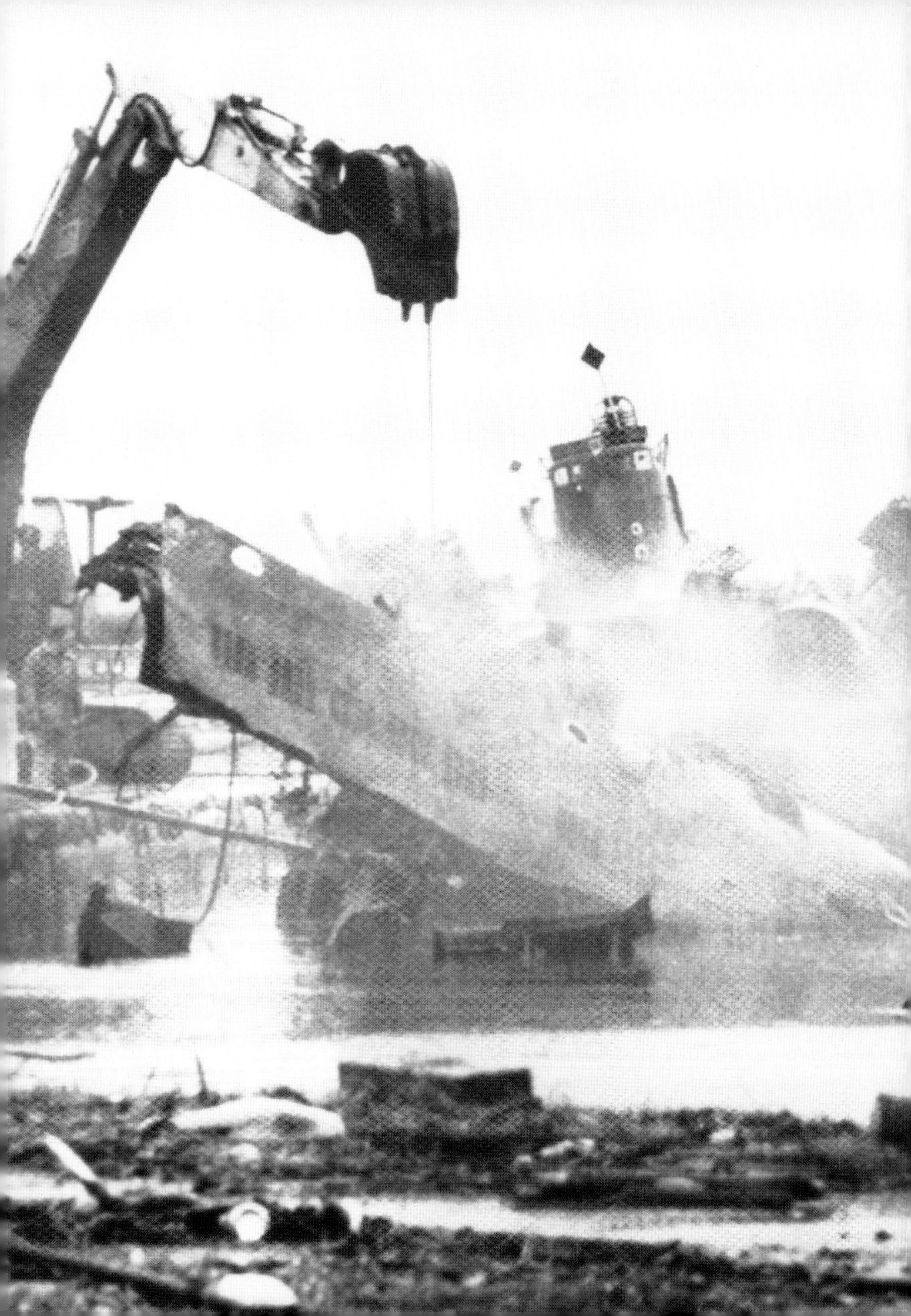

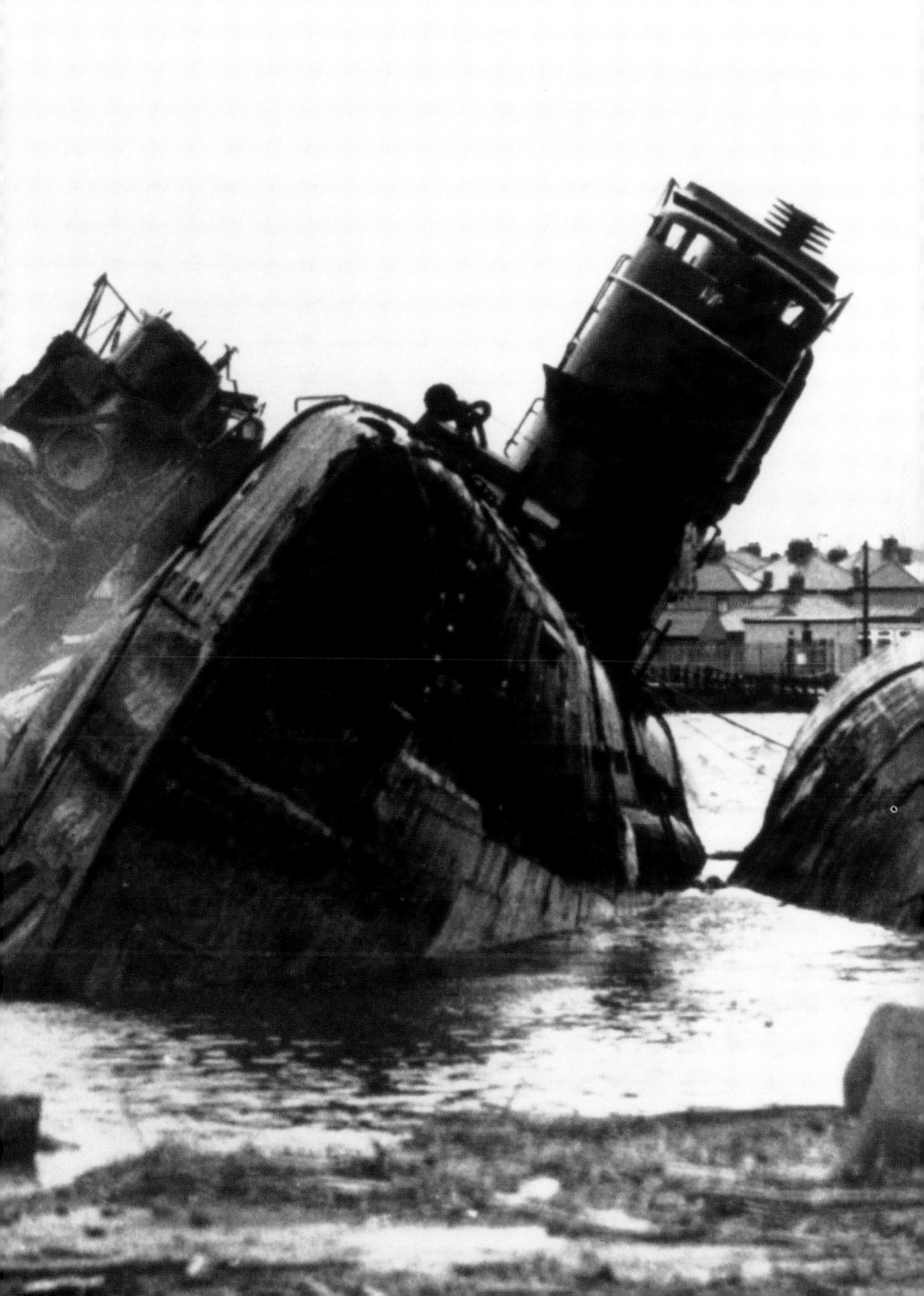

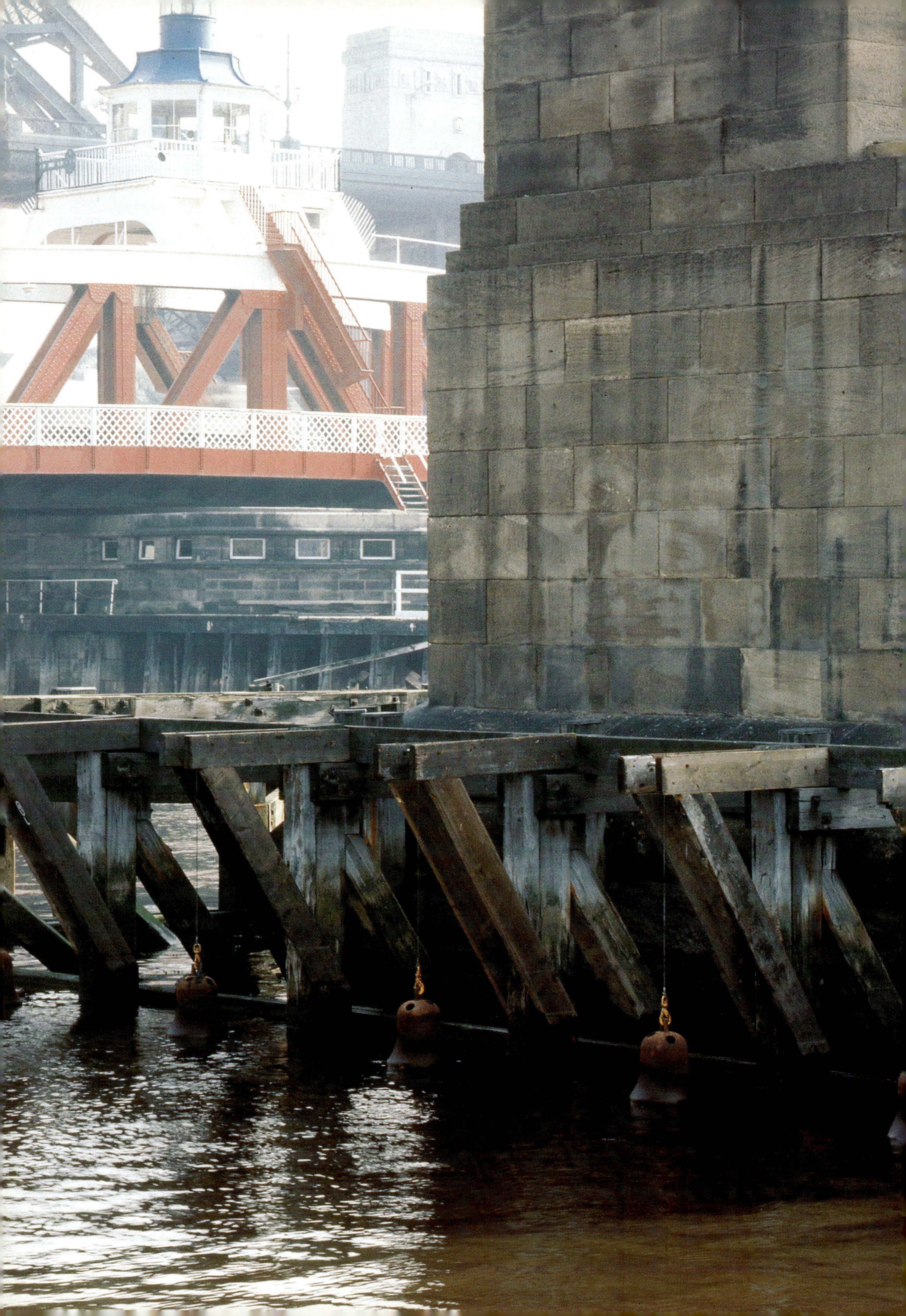

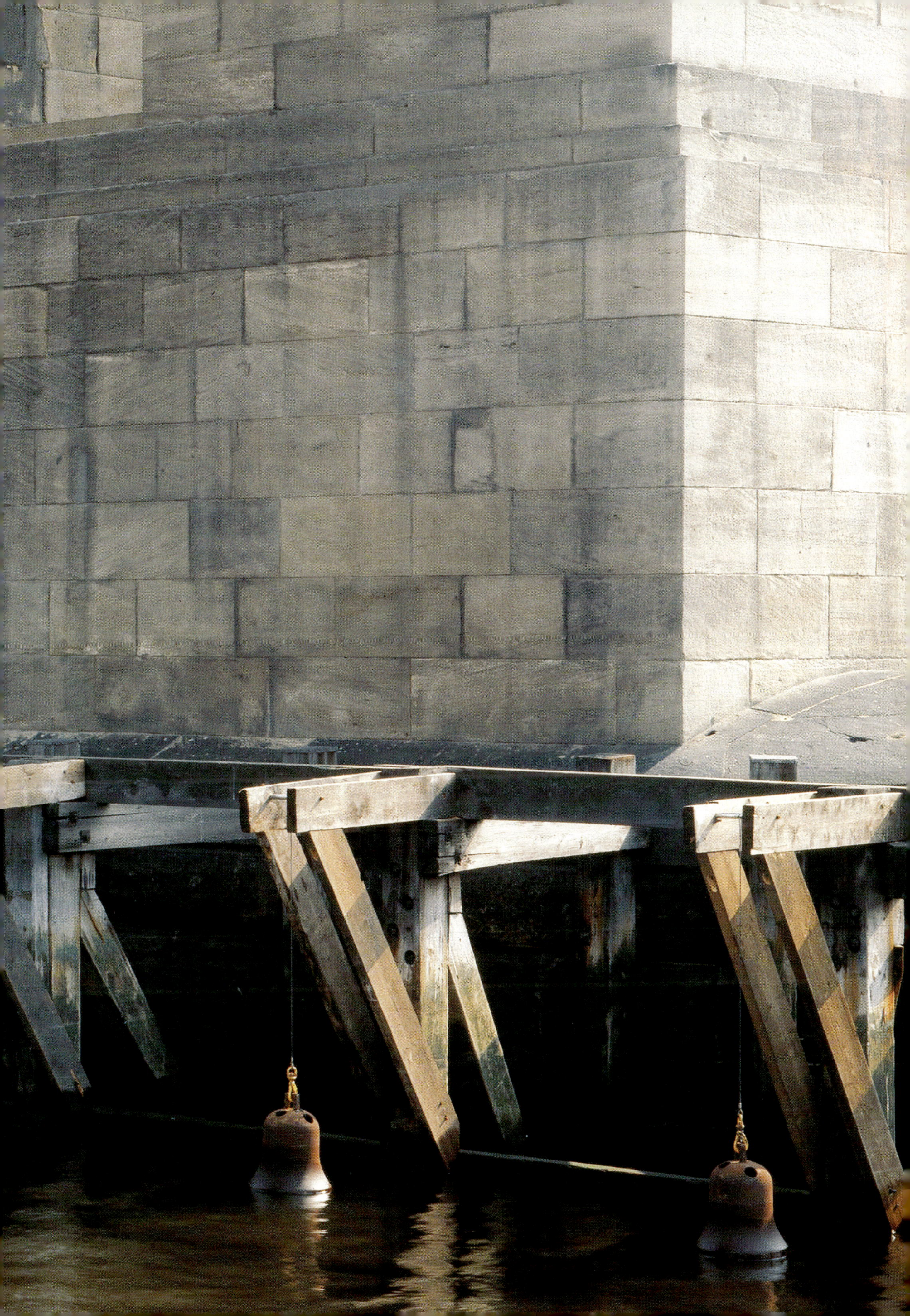

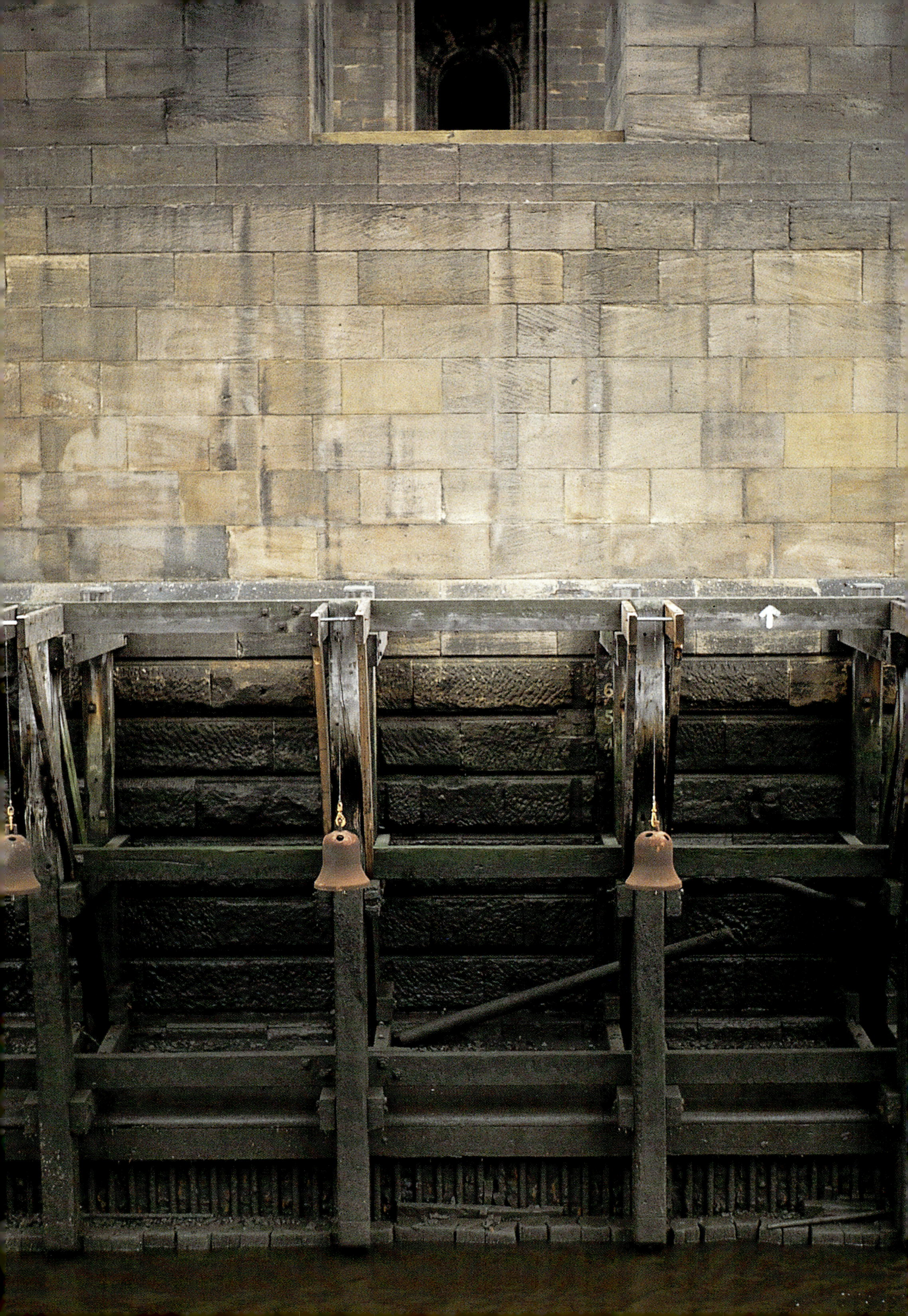

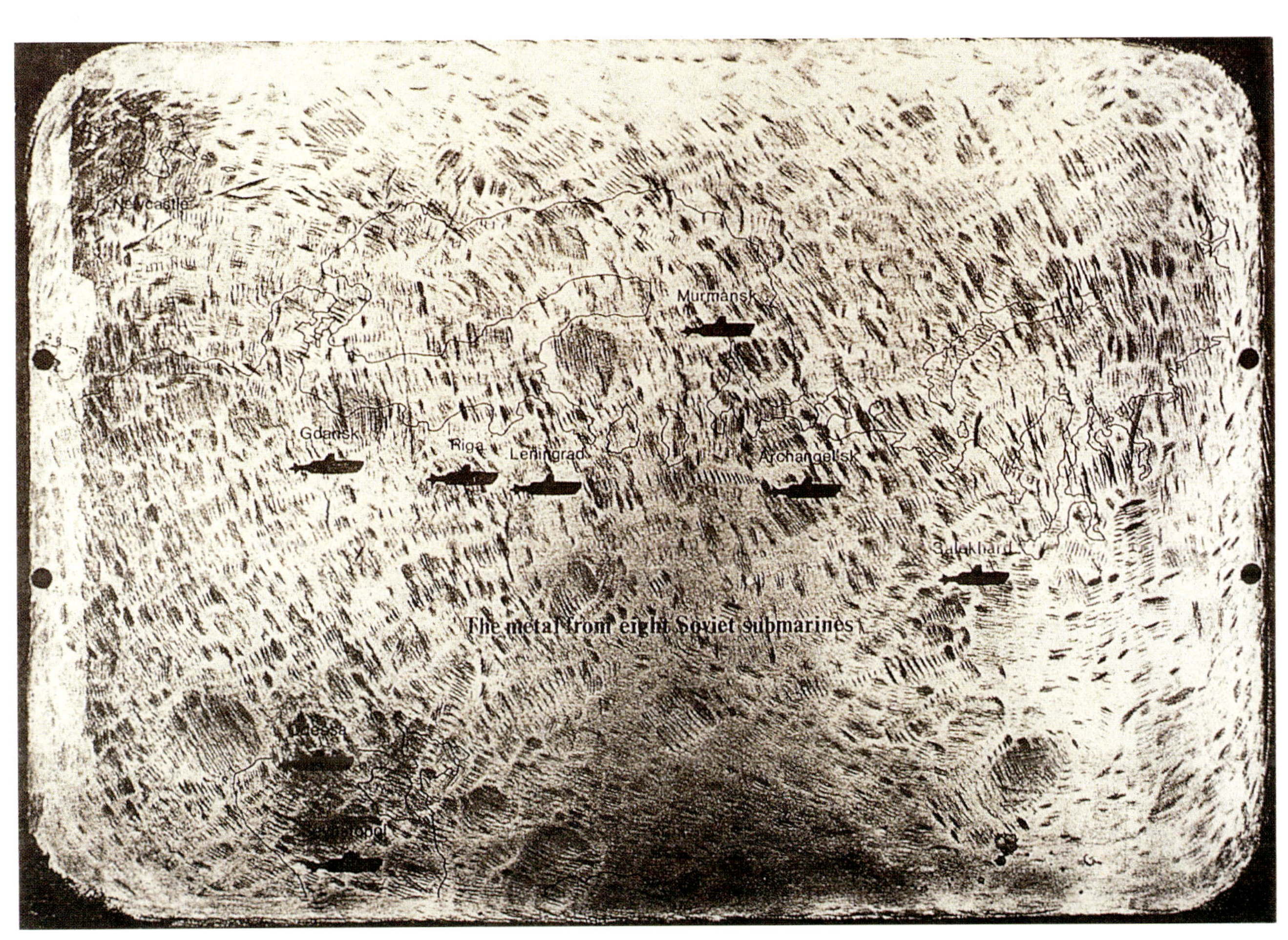

Preceding pages: *Trace Elements*, 1990
High Level Bridge,
Newcastle upon Tyne

Above: Steel plaque detailing eight
Soviet submarine ports

Detached Bell Tower

Detached Bell Tower developed *Trace Elements* by removing the bells to new contexts. For installations at Transmission Gallery, Glasgow; Ars 95, Helsinki and Orchard Gallery, Derry, the bells were tethered to beams and suspended around head height from low roofs (in Helsinki the site was an ammunition cellar), where they remained inert and visible. The choice of cities in Scotland, Finland and Northern Ireland was deliberate in each being coastal or river ports near national borders. In a poetic return, the steel from the eight submarines revisited locations near the Atlantic Sea, the North Sea and the Baltic.

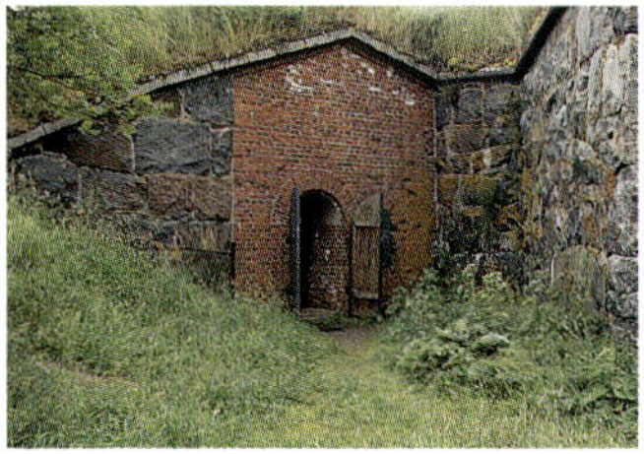

Entrance to Battery 2,
Suomenlinna, Finland

Opposite: *Detached Bell Tower*, 1995
Installed in Battery 2 Ammunitions
Cellar 18, Suomenlinna, Finland
Photography Antti Kuivalainen

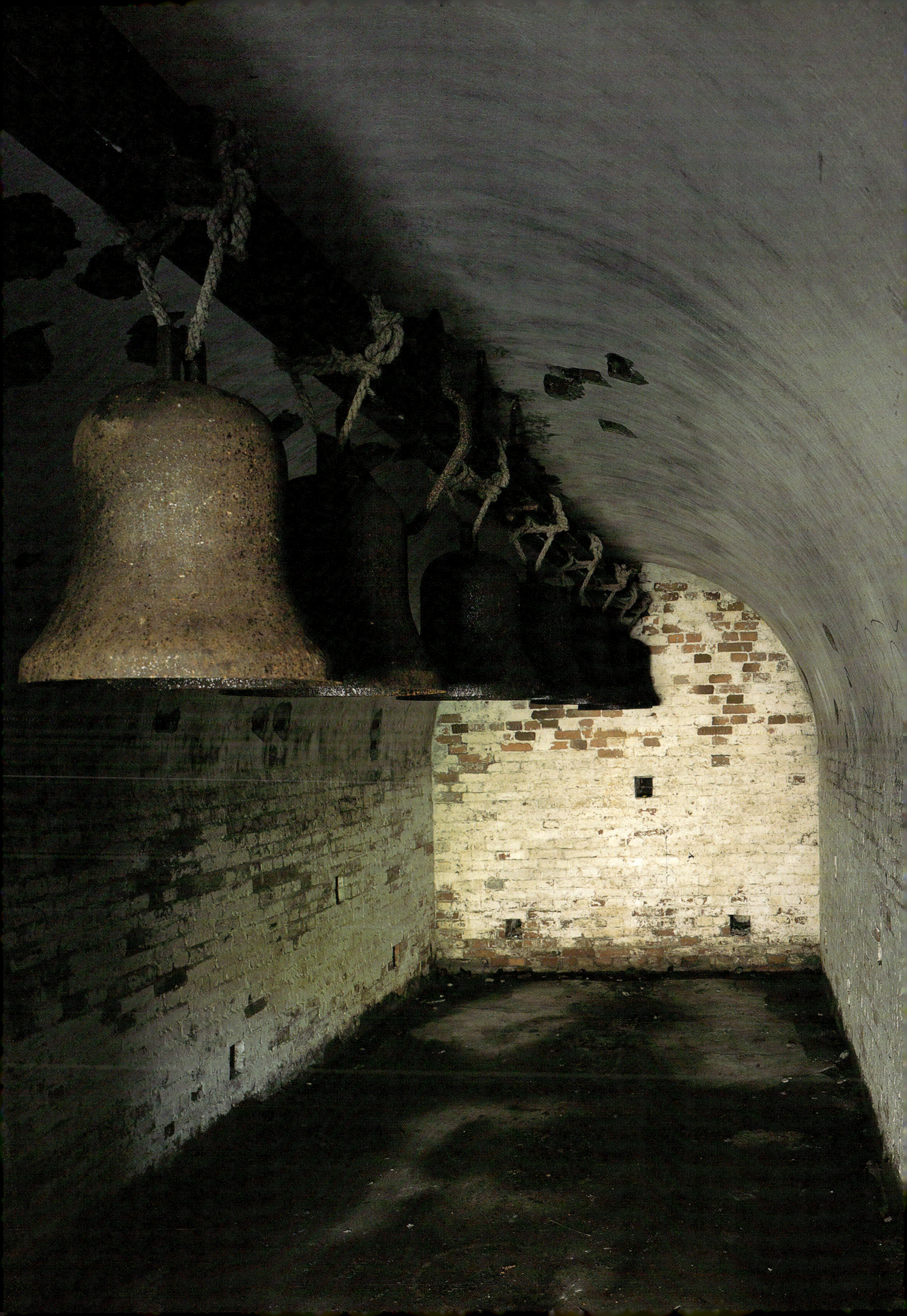

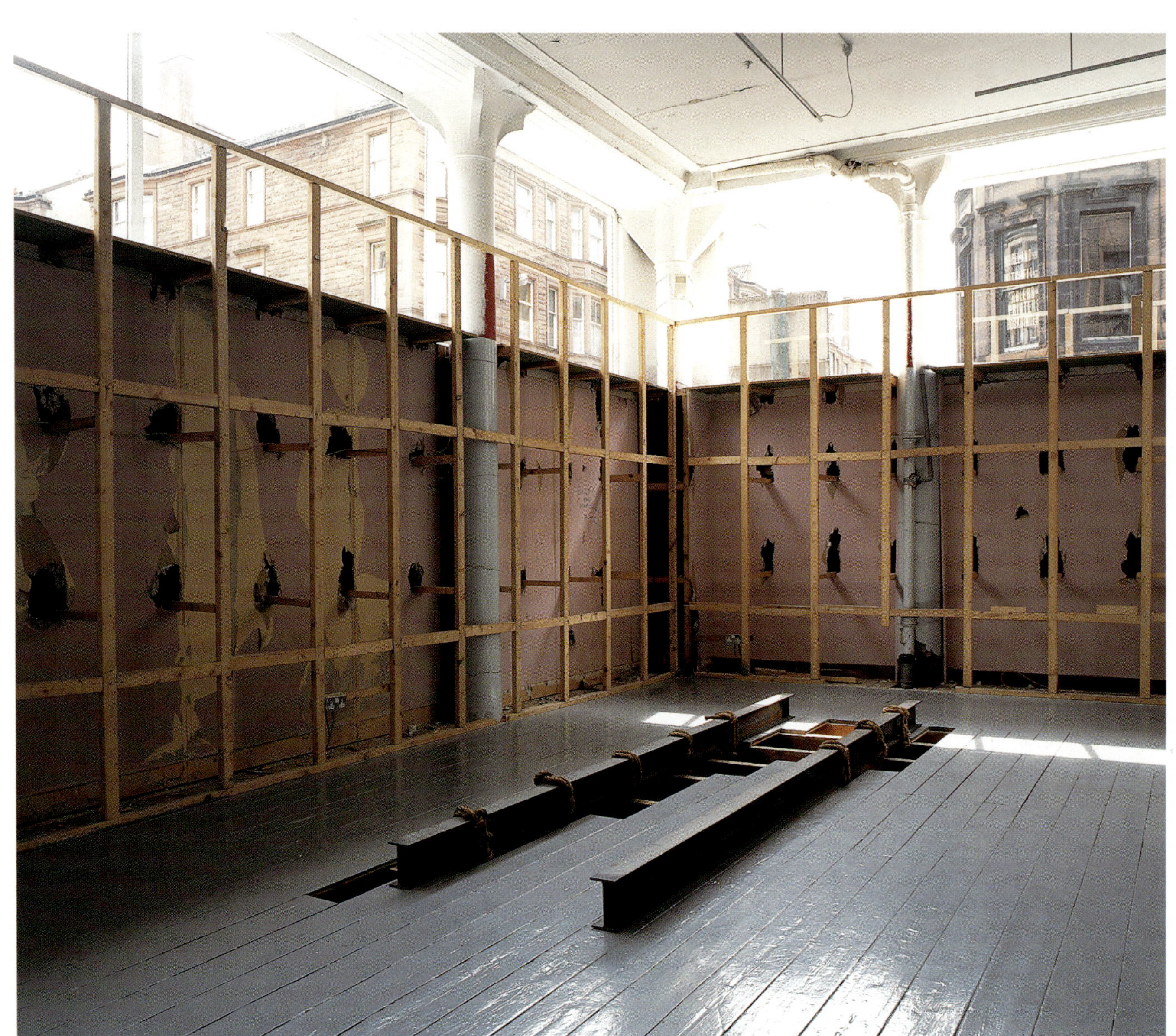

Opposite: *Detached Bell Tower*, 1994
Transmission Gallery, Glasgow
Installation view. (main gallery)
Photography Simon Starling

Below: *Detached Bell Tower*,
Transmission Gallery
Installation view. (basement)
Photography Simon Starling

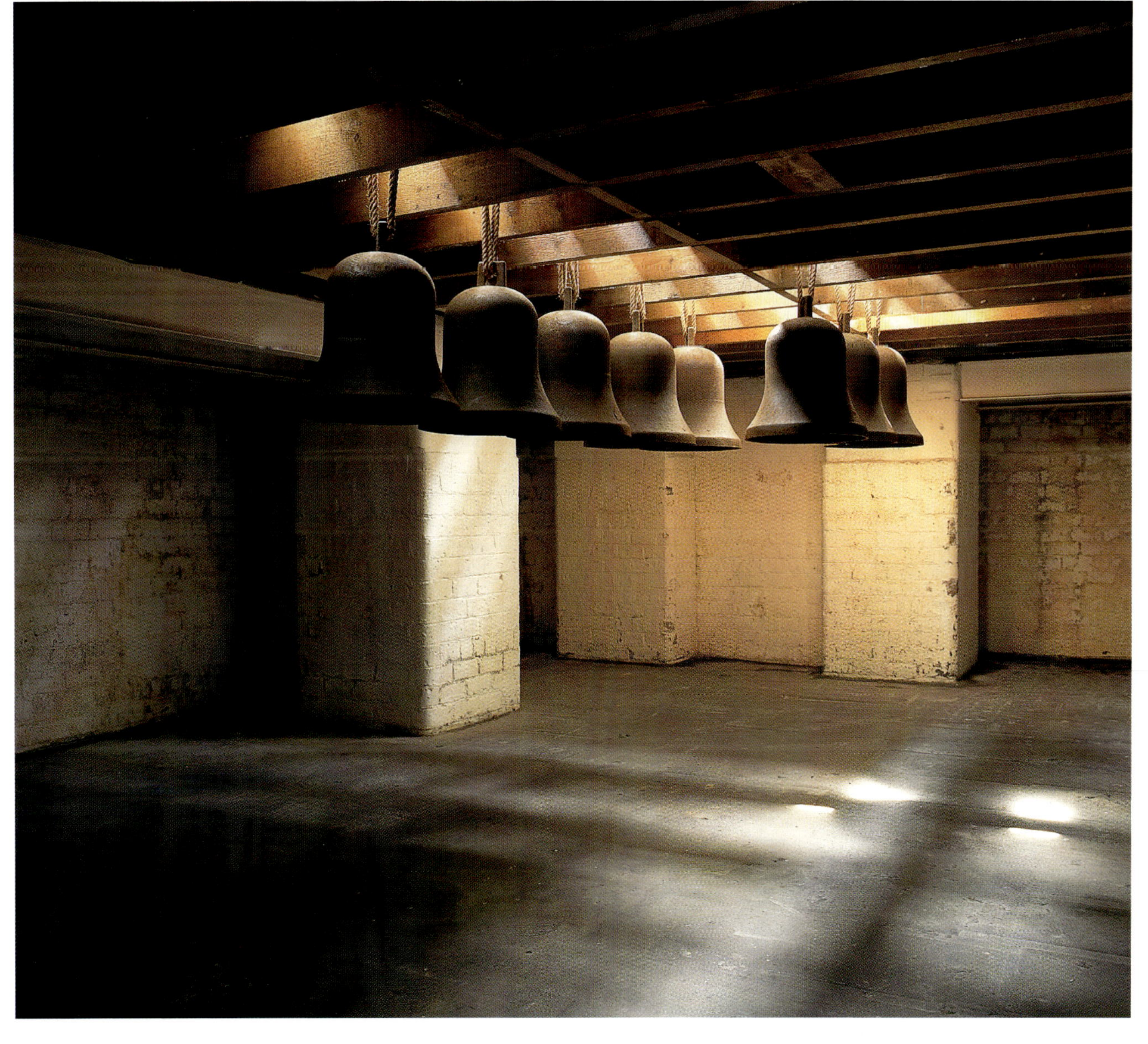

Buoy

Buoy is a major work featuring a characteristically large number of transformations. During the Cold War these submarines represented to the Western mind a dark, hidden and remote threat beneath the waves. By contrast, for those Soviets who worked on them (and coincidentally, Gec later learned that one of his Ukrainian cousins was a submariner) they provided a temporary home and a job.
But that was then. In the early 1990s the empty submarine carcasses, lying rusted and beached in the Blyth docks, were a fairly obvious sign of the dismantled and fragmented Soviet Bloc. The eight bells that formed *Detached Bell Tower* were melted down then installed as ballast into a fully operational buoy in 1996 and inaugurated in June of that year in Hartlepool at the Hartlepool Maritime Museum to become, initially, a land-based sculpture. Further locations were found, this time water based – thereby allowing the sculpture to operate as a functioning buoy – firstly near Belfast Lough (through The Commission of Irish Lights), and subsequently in the Irish Sea off Dublin. Many offshore sites are still being sought for *Buoy*, including Rotterdam, Reykjavik, Copenhagen, Oslo, Stockholm, Riga, St Petersburg and finally, the artist hopes, Murmansk (where the submarines started their commissions and which is now the submarine 'cemetery' of the Soviet Navy). All these locations, of course, retrace the routes of active Soviet submarines, and so will purposefully remark the old and redundant co-ordinates that once governed surreptitious movement underwater.

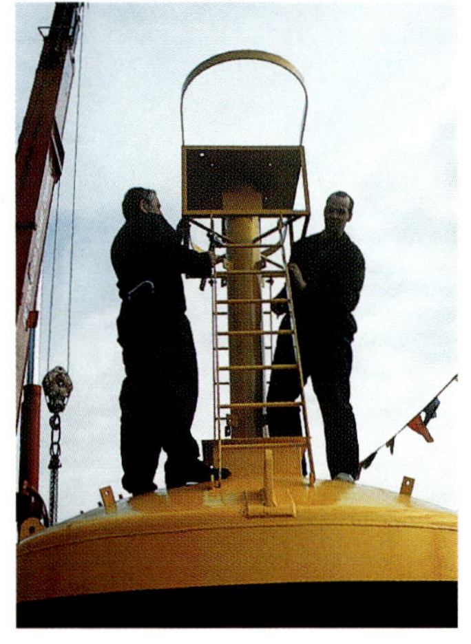

Maintenance work being carried out on *Buoy*

Opposite: *Buoy*, (maquette), 1996

Gec has spoken of wanting to place *Buoy* in the present, whilst acknowledging its past. Since the work's creation it has either been stored or brought out alongside other buoys to serve its intended utilitarian function, i.e. marking shipping lanes, dangerous marine objects or harbour entrances (each powerfully ironic functions considering the origin of the piece). After the siting in Belfast and Dublin, Gec started to plan an alteration to the work by placing advanced recording and sensing equipment on board, transforming it into a state-of-the-art marine weather station. Malevolent surveillance will be recast into benevolent service. This shift in role and function has not been fully achieved yet, and marks a future phase of the project which will occur through collaboration with the International Association of Lighthouse Authorities (the organisation responsible for buoyancy systems world-wide) and with the help of Trinity House, London (the central organisation for global positioning satellites and maritime navigation in England and Wales). The artist will work with the authorities to place *Buoy* in an experimental zone to begin tests, before its voyage continues.

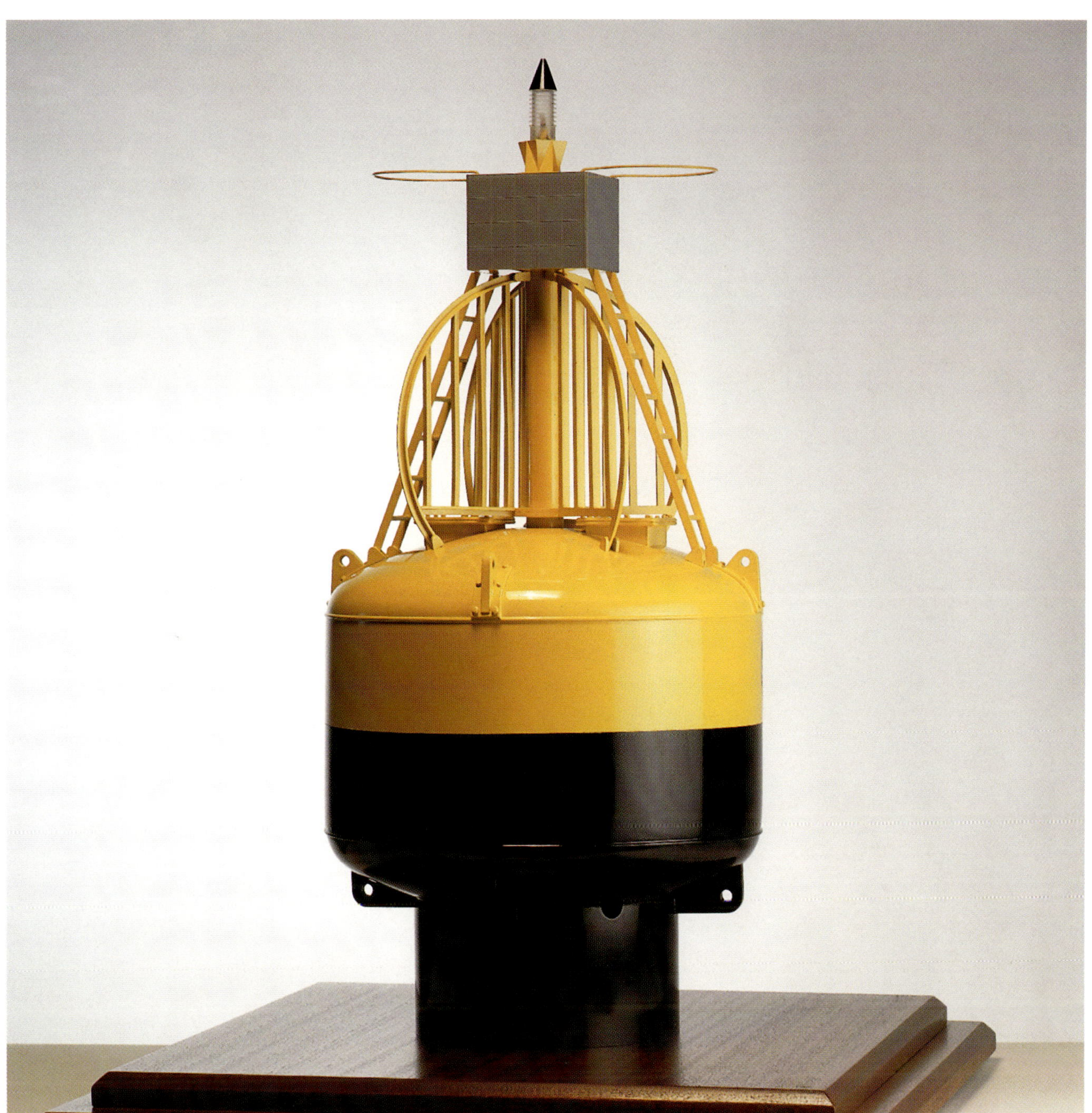

Buoy is 'site-specific art' that refuses to be tethered to its moorings. As with *Natural History*, the work is accruing different meanings with each repositioning. When it has been set in the sea as a temporary marker (denoted by its yellow and black markings) it is a fully functioning object among others, yet also at the same time an acknowledged sculpture in the broadest possible sense; it is an unremarkable co-ordinate for a sea captain who passes it in the sea, as well as an anecdotal point of contact for friends and helpers of the artist who wonder where it now lies. We might consider it in the context of Lucy Lippard's description of public art, as "Permanent or ephemeral, object and performance, preferably interdisciplinary, democratic, sometimes functional or didactic, a public art exists in the hearts, minds, ideologies and education of its audience as well as in their physical, sensuous experience."[13] It is a strong mental image, the buoy itself floating in a cold sea marking a real shipping lane, but within its form holding the recast metal of eight Soviet submarines. Even when, as now, it lies in store at Harwich there is a poetic, melancholic note struck as we wait for the next phase of the project to take form and lead to the re-release of *Buoy* into the oceans.

Technical drawings for *Buoy*, by Allister Welding Co

More than anything, though, *Buoy* acts as a symbolic marker for the two-way passages that lie between things, the mapped out abstractions that connect countries, communities or individuals with each other – trade routes, if you like, on a psycho-geographic plane. The linkages, the geometries of power, may be invisible to surface scrutiny but exist nevertheless. *Buoy* is not so much an 'artwork' or 'end product' as a series of ongoing activities, undertaken by the artist and others who come into contact with it (physically or mentally), that illuminates how parts of our world actually work. The history, which is almost alchemically embedded in the metal, cannot be extracted or removed. That which can be said of *Buoy* can also be said of *Natural History* or its predecessor *Bitter Waters* – physical as well as conceptual elements within the work may dissipate and spread with each transformation, but nothing truly disappears. The processes of submersion and dredging up take place all the time, without end.

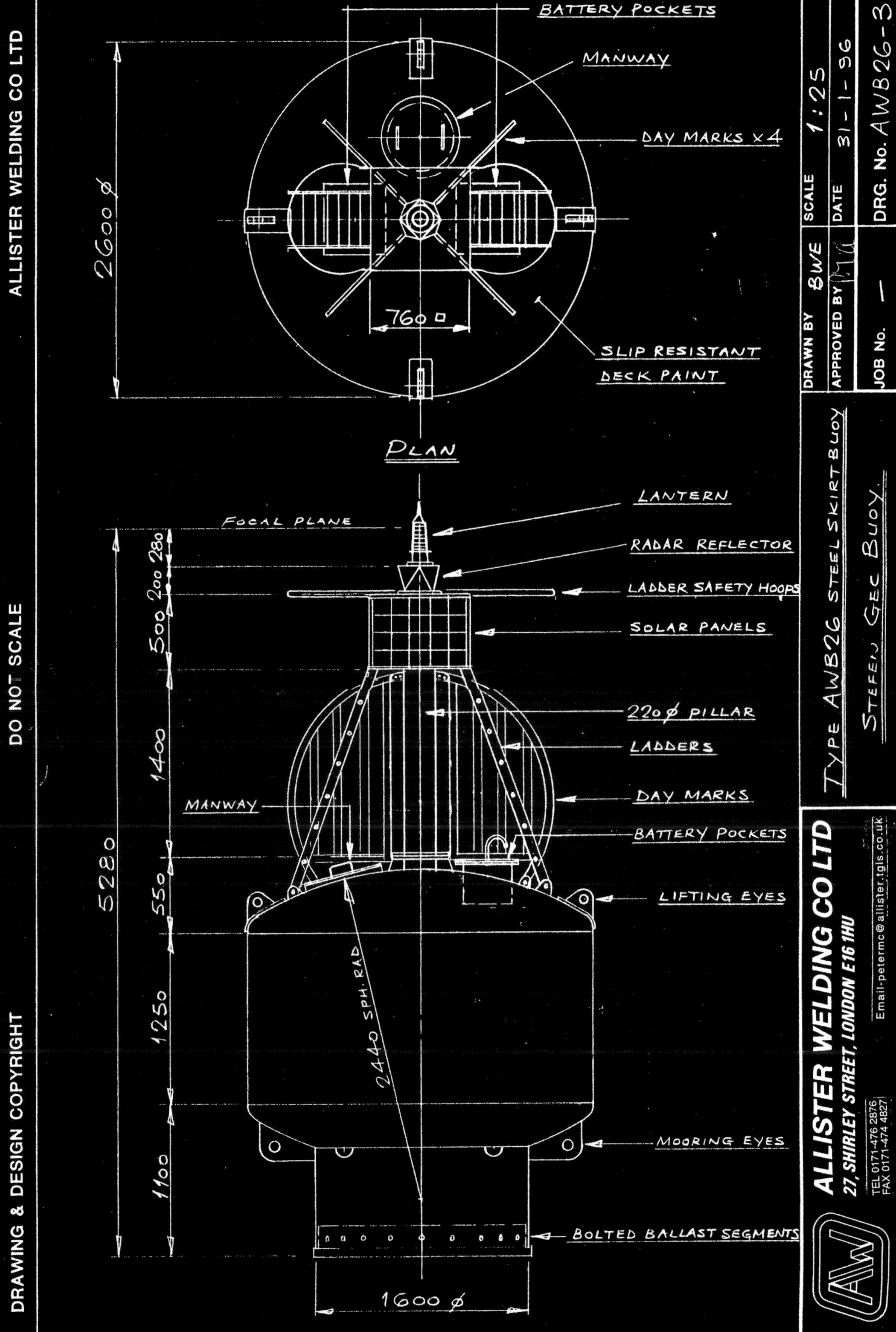

BATTERY POCKETS
MANWAY
DAY MARKS x4
SLIP RESISTANT
DECK PAINT
2600 ø
760 □
PLAN
FOCAL PLANE
LANTERN
RADAR REFLECTOR
LADDER SAFETY HOOPS
SOLAR PANELS
220ø PILLAR
LADDERS
DAY MARKS
MANWAY
BATTERY POCKETS
LIFTING EYES
MOORING EYES
BOLTED BALLAST SEGMENTS
2440 SPH. RAD
5280
280
200
500
1400
550
1250
1100
1600 ø
DRAWING & DESIGN COPYRIGHT
DO NOT SCALE
ALLISTER WELDING CO LTD
TYPE AWB26 STEEL SKIRT BUOY
DRAWN BY BWE
APPROVED BY
JOB No. 1
SCALE 1:25
DATE 31-1-96
DRG. No. AWB26-3
ALLISTER WELDING CO LTD
27, SHIRLEY STREET, LONDON E16 1HU
TEL 0171-476 2876
FAX 0171-474 4827

Buoy being constructed at
Allister Welding Co, London

Opposite: *Buoy* in Belfast Lough, 1997

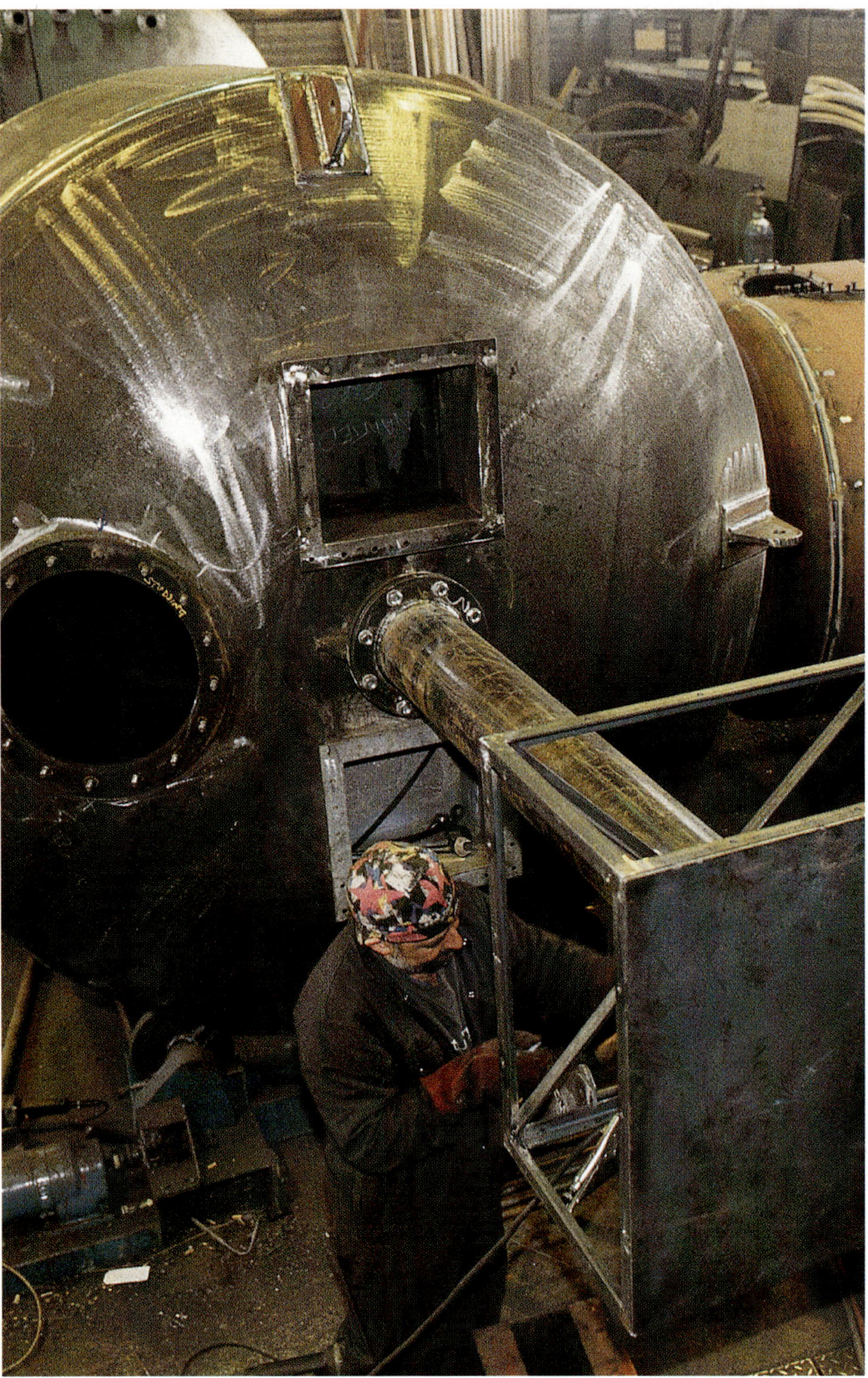

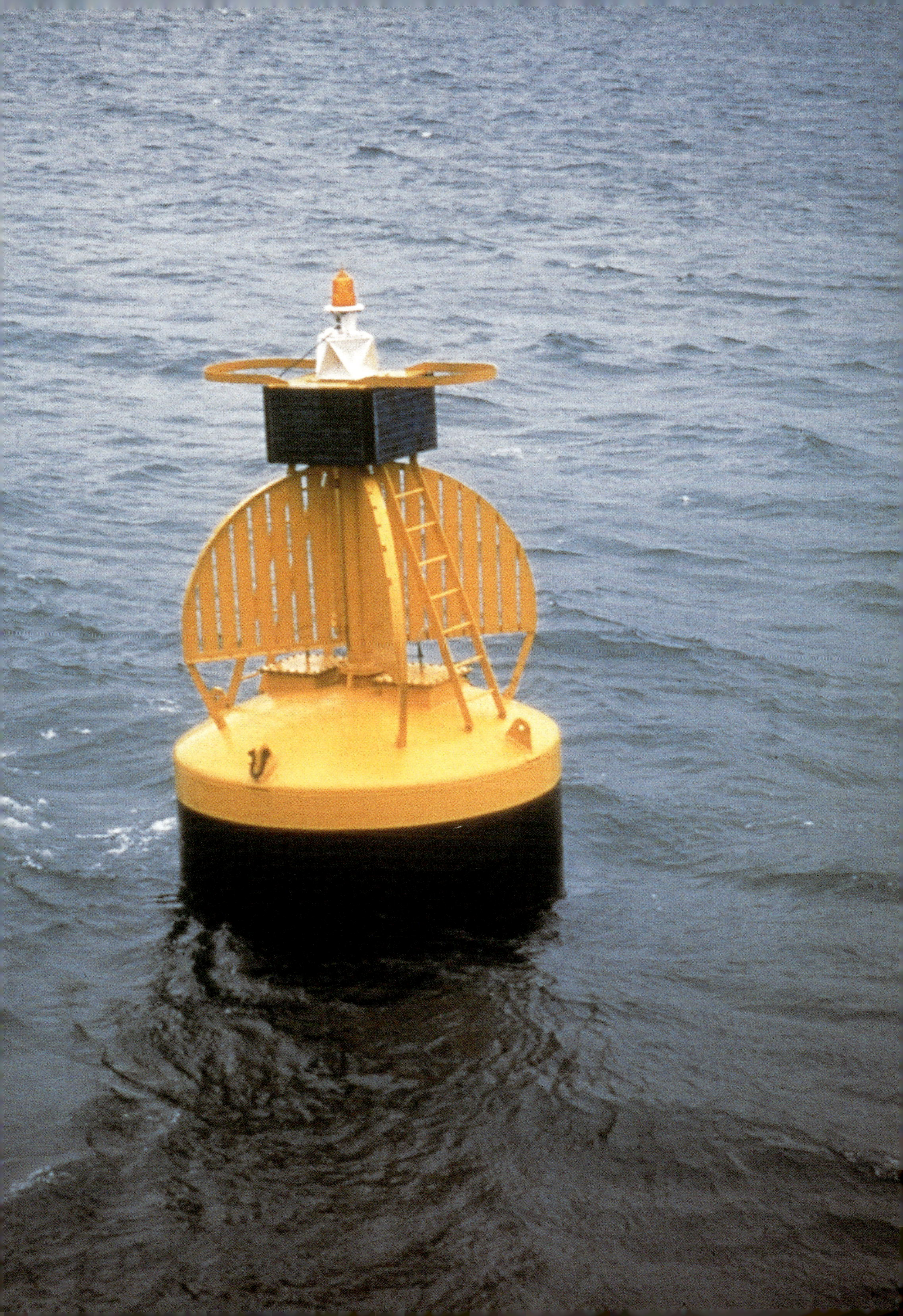

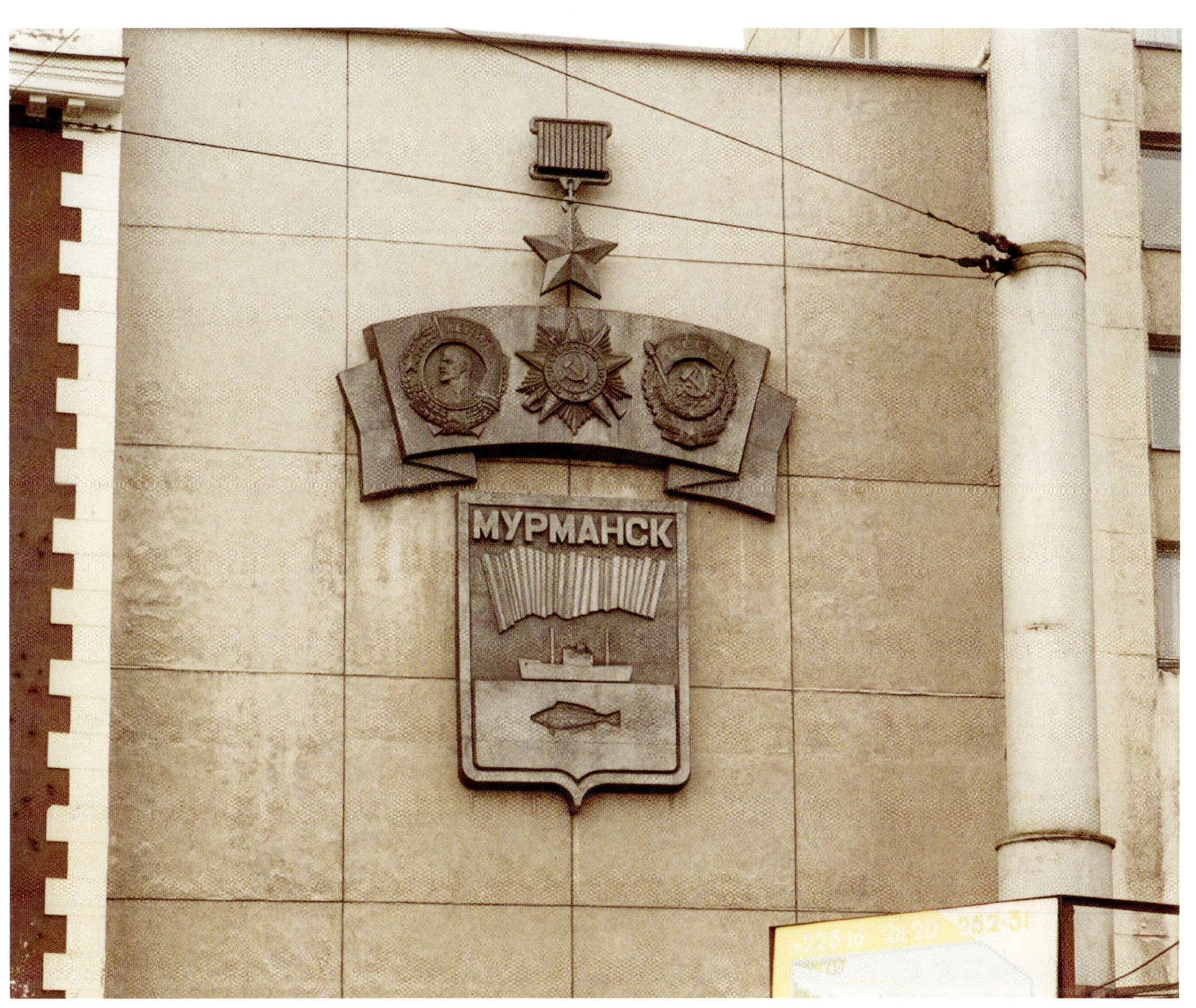
МУРМАНСК

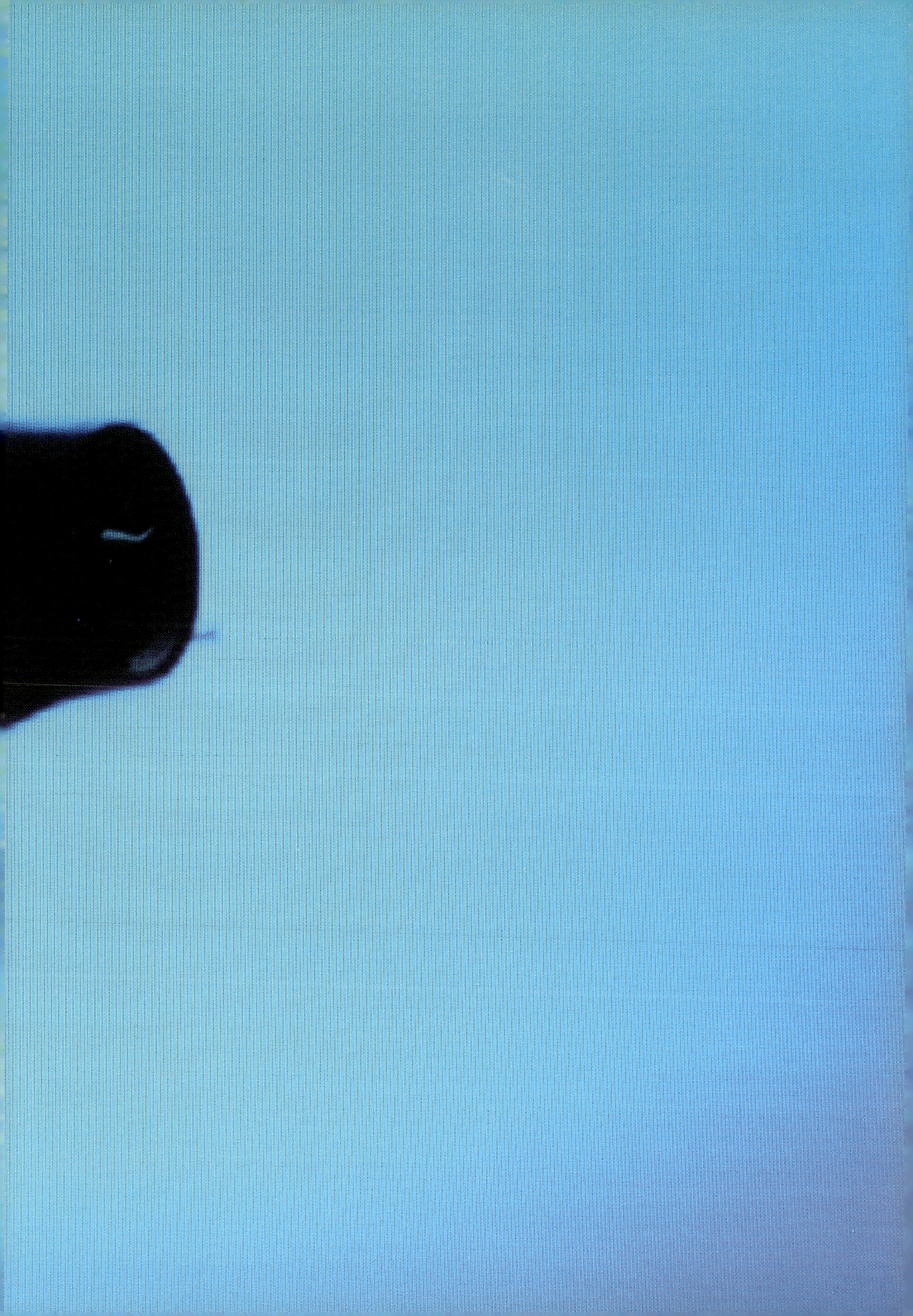

Towards a New Public Domain

Perhaps a new type of art is becoming possible; one which takes its place in an expanded public domain. This art adopts and develops some of the rethinking that is taking place in other disciplines, across the physical and social sciences in particular, whilst remaining affirmatively visual and artistic. By pushing further the already broad definition of what a contemporary sculptor might be, it is becoming possible for some practitioners to create objects that operate in the world with a distinct difference from conventional sculpture and installation art. These works, rather than generating ideas directly through the visual alone, serve also to activate the space between objects, highlighting social integration, change and exchange as facts. Gec might be seen as an artist interested far more in a practice rooted in 'connectedness' rather than in essences; not through a kind of bland interdisciplinarity, but from a practice which builds from the direct experience of many communities, transformed through art. This is obviously not a social science, but a poetic, abstract even oppositional occupation, which weaves its way through the fabric of our lives. Gec seems to recognise instinctively that his work involves a move from the personal, private, specific and local towards the transparent, public and national; a kind of transition which Hannah Arendt captures well: "Since our feeling for reality depends utterly on appearance and therefore upon the existence of a public realm into which things can appear out of a darkness of sheltered existence, even the twilight which illuminates our private and intimate lives is ultimately derived from the much harsher light of the public realm." [14]

In the introduction reference was made to global situations and the extent to which they provide a determining context for the way in which Gec works. Mention was made to monolithic meanings that have to be broken down, or made light, through art. As well as the dialogue that Gec encourages between weight and lightness, there is the more obvious one between surface and depth – the dialogue between material that is presented to our gaze as finished work and what lies behind the work, available to explore if we wish. The image of the submarine, which as we have seen reoccurs in many works, particularly *Fragment* / 𝔙𝔢𝔫𝔤𝔢𝔞𝔫𝔠𝔢, is an eloquent metaphor for the surface / depth axis.

One of the great achievements of Gec's work is that it addresses some of the central issues of our modern age but manages to avoid vagueness, opacity and weight with respect to how these concerns are embodied as art. International conflicts between Eastern and Western cultures, migration of peoples, and the imaginary quality of transglobal communities are all subjects that interest many artists working today, as they do Gec. However, it is easy to illustrate the power of these issues and, if one is not careful, to bring art stillborn and inert into the world. Gec avoids this through the formal and conceptual stripping down of his practice, as evidenced in major works, each of which have a crystalline quality, accumulating complex meanings whilst being paradoxically simple in form and articulation. In essence, the bringing about of lightness, rather than weight, is a way of verifying and representing the world differently, and making it available to the imagination rather than to politics or economics alone.

Notes

1. Said, Edward, *Culture and Imperialism*, (1993), London: Vintage, 1994, p. 377

2. Said, *Culture and Imperialism*, p. xxviii

3. Said, *Culture and Imperialism*, p. 271

4. Hannerz, Ulf, *Transnational Connections Culture, people, places*, London and New York: Routledge, 1996, p. 8

5. Calvino, Italo, *Six Memos for the Next Millennium The Charles Eliot Norton Lectures 1985-6*, (trans. Patrick Creagh), London: Vintage, 1993, p. 97

6. McGonagle, Declan, 'New Transactions', *in Decadent Public Art: Contentious Term and Contested Practice*, David Harding and Pavel Büchler (eds.), Glasgow: Foulis Press, 1997, pp. 24-25

7. Said, *Culture and Imperialism*, p. 374

8. Arendt, Hannah, *The Human Condition*, Chicago and London: University of Chicago Press, 1958, pp. 90-91

9. Le Noury's opening address at the 2nd international congress of geographical sciences, 1875, quoted in Said, *Culture and Imperialism*, p. 205

10. Melville, Herman, *Moby Dick*, (1851), Harmondsworth: Penguin, 1972, p. 103

11. Entirely coincidentally, it transpired that in an early proposal for *Fædm*, Gec intended to read passages from Moby Dick over a 24 hour period in one of the decompression chambers in Plymouth. The idea was later superseded.

12. Gec, Stefan, *Trace Elements. Works from 1989-1995*, Derry and Newcastle: Orchard Gallery and Locus+, 1995, p. 30

13. In Harding and Büchler, *Decadent*, p. 6

14. Arendt, *The Human Condition*, p. 51

Much of the factual material and aesthetic intentions discussed above are based on a number of interviews conducted by the author with the artist over a five year period. The text here draws particularly on an interview conducted on 30 November 2001.

Projects UK was an arts organisation established in Newcastle upon Tyne in 1982 by two former members of the Basement Group, Ken Gill and Jon Bewley. Projects UK was the first arts organisation in the UK that operated solely from an office with no exhibition facilities. Its programme was context or site specific, temporary public artworks.

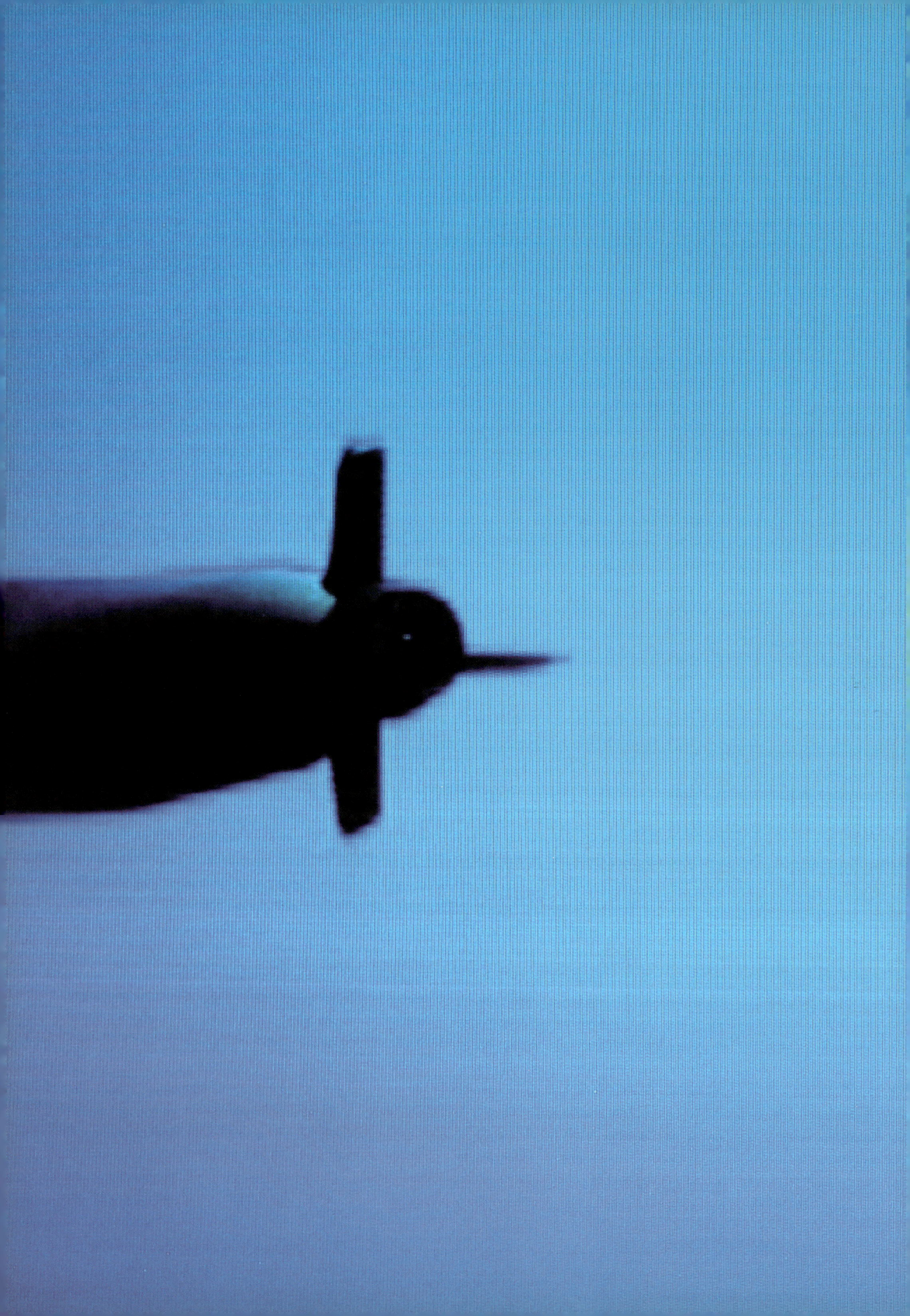

For Michael, Liam and Mira.

The artist would like to thank the many people who assisted in the realisation of the works included in this book, in particular Jon Bewley, Irene Faith and Andrew Patrizio.

www.stefangec.com

Edited by Jon Bewley

Designed by Gavin Ambrose

Printed in the European Union

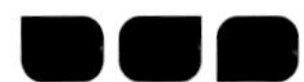

Architecture Art Design Fashion History Photography Theory and Things

Black Dog Publishing Limited

5 Ravenscroft Street
London
E2 7SH
UK

T 44 020 7613 1922
F 44 020 7613 1944
E info@bdp.demon.co.uk

British Library Cataloguing-in-Publication Data.

A catalogue record for this book is available from the British Library.

ISBN: 1 901033 43 0

This publication has been commissioned by Barrow-in-Furness Borough Council Public Art Programme. Funded by The Arts Council of England, Northern Arts, Heart of Barrow Single Regeneration Budget.

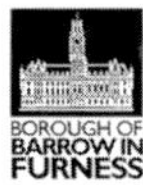

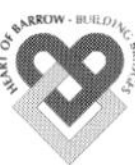

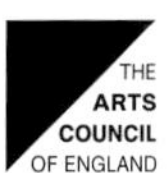

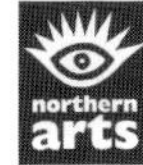